A FATHERLESS
CURIOSITY

A Fatherless Curiosity

www.phenomenallybecoming.com

tyra@phenomenallybecoming.com

IG tyra_d_james

Twitter @tyradj11

Facebook: Tyra James, & Tyra James Transformational Life Coach

Publisher: Kim Roundtree

ISBN: 9798394245916

TABLE OF CONTENTS

A **FATHERLESS** CURIOSITY

Tyra D. James
Visionary

Serign Marong

Damarius Bilbo

Therome James

William Logan

Daniel Vasquenza

Juan Alarcon

Richard Quisenberry

Mark McClintock

Troy Cromer

Micheal Dorris

Vincent Alan Rhodes

James E. Keys

Alexander Pezo

Abdur Karim

Kenneth Swan Jr.

C. Derek Easterling

Kevin Montgomery

Emery Williams Jr.

Lawrence U. Lane

Dwayne Archbold

Dwayne was born and raised in the Crown Heights section of Brooklyn, New York. He attended P.S 161 Elementary School and Atwell I.S 61 Middle School, where he began his journey to becoming a basketball player. As a young man, he became more aware of his surroundings, his eyes were opened, and his thoughts became more his own. His transition during those three years from a kid to a young man was exciting. For the first time, his experiences were not systematic but involved his choices. His four high school years are where his personality and character would further develop. Dwayne's years at Paul Robeson High School were life changing. He began as a fourteen-year-old freshman who didn't know anyone but left with people who, through the years, became family, creating bonds that would forever tie them together.

Paul Robeson High had ten Division I basketball players within a four-year period. After graduating, Dwayne left as an All-City player and was heavily scouted by colleges and universities. Accepting a full scholarship to Siena College was gratifying but also nerve-wracking for Dwayne as he would be leaving family and "the familiar" behind for the first time. Nevertheless, Dwayne adapted to the new environment and overcame many obstacles. He successfully graduated from Siena as a top basketball prospect and even held the NCAA conference tournament record for most points scored for ten years.

Foreword

By Dwayne Archbold

I learned of Tyra James through my wife, Tennille, participating in Tyra's Phenomenally Becoming Book Club. Tennille immensely enjoyed the book club and spoke often and highly of Tyra and the positive impact on her personally, combined with the camaraderie amongst the ladies, shared experiences, and the uniqueness of the book club. A few months after Tennille joined the book club, I met Tyra and her husband, Therome (TJ), at the book club's first scholarship dinner. The event served as a  dual celebration in honor of the *A'spe* magazine issue launch and the cover reveal featuring Tyra and Therome as "A True Power Couple," celebrating 25 years of marriage. Needless to say, there was an instant connection, and they've become close family friends.

Fast forward to four years later, when Tyra sent me a text stating she wanted to share something with me and asked if I had time for a conversation. Of course, I agreed. When I later received the phone call from Tyra and TJ, after our normal short meaningful conversation, Tyra asked if she could ask me a personal question. I paused and said, "Sure." What was the personal question? "How are you doing as a father?"

Following my response, Tyra mentioned that she had observed me as a father and felt I was a great father. She then shared her personal story and the impetus and intention for this anthology on fatherhood, a matter which is near and dear to her heart. She then asked if I would consider participating in the project by writing the Foreword. After careful consideration, I accepted.

I was raised in a two-parent household and was lucky to know the feeling of having a father who lived his role and responsibilities. I was, however, also aware of fathers who either didn't know how to be, could not be or chose not to be a part of the foundation that could help mold their children. At 17, I became a father myself. I quickly began to realize the word *father* would have a different meaning for everyone. Not everyone would embrace the true meaning of the word father.

In this book, you will learn the challenges, rewards, experiences, highs, and lows of fatherhood, but most importantly, what led to the writers' understanding of their role as a father. The authentic and transparent stories from childhood to fatherhood are varied. The book covers it all - men who knew of their father but had little to no connection; fathers that lived outside of the household, some close and some far away; fathers that came around often or lived in the home, but a bond was or was not formed; and fathers that had or still have a significant impact in their lives. The stories are heartfelt, raw, gripping, revealing, relatable, and inspiring. You will not leave empty! These unique experiences will provide an understanding of how the long-term effect on these individuals made them into the fathers they are today. However, and without question, the intention of this powerful anthology is to create a movement that brings value and evokes change. It begins with unmasking the truth of fatherhood and its expectations (spoken and unspoken), joys, ups and downs, pressures, happiness, responsibilities, challenges, fears, and rewards.

This stirring yet empowering book is unique for two reasons – the vision and curiosity of a female provoked the conversation and created this project, and a group of 21 men courageously shared their truths to the question, "How are you doing as a father?" It will leave you reflecting on the long-term effects of your childhood with or without your father and its impact on your life's journey. You, too, will be challenged to answer the very personal question: "How are you doing as a father?"

Dennis Jolley

Dennis Jolley was born in West Germany, while his father served in Vietnam. Soon after, his family moved to the south Atlanta area. Before starting high school, his parents moved him and his two brothers to north metro Atlanta. Dennis' love for reading led him to a career in education. He has taught English at all levels of high school, a metro Atlanta technical college, and a local university. He currently teaches at-risk middle and high school students in the metro Atlanta area. Dennis is married and is blessed with an amazing daughter. He is excited that he will soon be a grandfather.

Preface

By Dennis Jolley

"Train up a child in the way he should go, and when he is old, he will not depart from it."

~ Proverbs 22:6 NKJV

It has been said time and again that having a child doesn't make someone a father. While this has become cliché, there is so much truth within this seemingly simple statement. Becoming a father is easy, but choosing to be the father a child needs is incredibly difficult. All too often, we forget that men were once little boys struggling to navigate the path to manhood. Some are blessed with proper role models, while others grow up without someone to guide them down the circuitous road of life. Experiences during  a young man's formative years can have a lasting ripple effect that can span generations.

A Fatherless Curiosity is a collection of stories by men from all walks of life who have come together to share their incredible stories about their relationship with their fathers and the lessons they've learned from raising their own children. Some have grown up in loving families with dads who taught them how to become men, while others share memories of growing up in a home without a loving father. As they reveal deeply personal information, these men show us how important fathers are in the development of their children. Remembering their stories requires them to pull back the façade and reveal the heartwarming and gut-wrenching truths they lived. The stories they tell about their upbringing are crucial for us to gain insight into what led them to understand just how important they are in their children's lives. And it is our hope these stories will help shine the light of guidance on a younger generation while also encouraging struggling dads to look into their story, gain clarity and begin the journey to healing within themselves and with their children.

No matter the journey we take, each of our stories is unique, and as children, we aren't equipped with an understanding of the world around us, so we must rely on our parents to guide us until we are capable of navigating on our own. Once we've emerged into adulthood and become fathers, we must decide if we are going to continue to live for our own pursuits or put our needs aside and live for the child who calls us Daddy. The choice we make will have monumental consequences for everyone involved.

While some offer unconditional love and support for their children, many perpetuate the cycle of an absent or unloving father. Thankfully, millions of men have been able to deal with the brokenness of their childhood home and overcome the demons of the past to chart a better course for their children. This, however, doesn't come without many slips and falls along the way, but time and again, they take the memories of their own experiences and devote their entire lives to being the father their child so desperately needs.

The men sharing their stories about becoming fathers and the trials and tribulations that came with fatherhood is special. Whether they are the biological father or not is inconsequential because these men chose to be the best father they could be because of or despite their individual experiences with their own fathers. As these fathers remember the past to make sense of what it means to be a father in the present, they share stories that will show openly that no man is an island. Their life experiences as children shaped the men they would eventually become.

Some will show us joyful moments, while others open their hearts and allow us to experience their incredibly painful memories. Either way, by God's grace, they were able to grow and learn what it means to become the role model their children deserve. This maturity allows this generation of men to be a living example by training their sons how to behave toward women and impress upon their daughters the expectations they should set for their future husbands.

There are no perfect fathers, yet these men have made peace with the missteps and victories along the way and understand the hard work it takes to become the best father they can be. The combination of mistakes and successes pushes them forward. Our greatest hope is that the stories they tell will help encourage fathers already on the journey and new fathers alike to do everything in their power to make their children a priority.

No matter how tough life can be, one thing is for sure. Each man knows there is a Father in heaven who loves him more than we can ever imagine. And through God's grace, kindness, love, and mercy, all fathers have the opportunity to share those same virtues with their children. When all else fails, we can look to God's word for the answers to all our questions, and when you feel you may be falling short, our Heavenly Father is a simple prayer away. After all, He sent His son to save us all.

We can't choose who our fathers are, nor can we change how we were treated by them. We can, however, choose how we allow them to shape us. By learning this simple lesson, we can treat our children the way God expects us to, and, in turn, we can choose how we shape them.

A Fatherless Curiosity will be a source of refuge when the struggles of fatherhood arise. Enlightened fathers will help our sons and daughters shape their children while allowing the lessons we've learned as fathers to help us become even better grandfathers. This will be the legacy we leave for generations to come.

Tyra D. James

Master Transformational Life Coach,

Keynote Speaker, Author, Vision Board Strategist

A powerful, positive, and larger-than-life force of personality, Tyra James brings a special brand of evolving and wholeness to her life coaching business. Tyra is a master at teaching others to live the greater version of themselves and creating the life they dream of. She is a Master Transformational Life Coach and is an empowering, informational, and transformational facilitator, speaker, and seminar presenter. Tyra received her life coaching certifications from The Life Coach Institute (LCI) and The International Coaching Science Research Foundation and has a successful Life Coaching business in Kennesaw, Georgia (Phenomenally Becoming Coaching & Consulting)

Tyra specializes in Personal and Professional Development, Marriage and Relationship Coaching, and Creating a Powerful Vision for her clients. Tyra is gifted at providing revelatory information, the impetus for life-changing transformation. A Vision Board Strategist, she teaches the laws and concepts of creating a powerful vision board. She is a master at teaching others to learn, implement, create, and manifest the life they truly want and desire. She has had countless opportunities to teach this to the masses, including Non-Profit Organizations, Schools, Churches, Fortune Five Hundred Companies, the NFL, and Celebrities. In addition to her successful Life Coaching business, Tyra is the creator and founder of the Phenomenally

Becoming Book Club and Dinner Gathering, where she provides a space for women to express their love for reading and leading; a Certified Practical Parent Facilitator; and holds a Personal Training Certification from America Council on Exercise (ACE).

Tyra has always been active in her community, including formerly serving and holding The Health Chair position for the Sandusky Branch of NAACP, and a former member of the National Council of Negro Women. In 2011 she received the "Woman of the Year" award for her exemplary service to the community. As an accomplished businesswoman, in 2012, Tyra collaborated with T.O.P.S. INC (Training on Prevention Services) and was named Co-City Leader for the youth tutoring program for the city of Sandusky. Tyra is the wife of Therome James for 29 years, and together they have a 27-year-old daughter Logan James. She is most grateful for the gift that God has given her to relate, inspire and empower others.

Tyra James
www.phenomenallybecoming.com
tyra@phenomenallybecoming.com
IG tyra_d_james
Twitter @tyradj11
Facebook: Tyra James, & Tyra James Transformational Life Coach

Introduction

By Tyra D. James

From the Visionary...

The important thing is not to stop questioning. Curiosity has its own reason for existing. One cannot help but be in awe when one contemplates the mysteries of eternity, of life, and of the marvelous structure of reality. It is enough if one tries to comprehend only a little of this mystery every day.

Albert Einstein

Dear Reader,

***W**hy is curiosity so powerful?* Here's my take on it. The power of curiosity comes from its ability to help us all learn and grow. Curiosity prevents us from becoming obsolete, fills in our many blind spots, and causes us to thirst and improve our self-awareness; at least, this is what it has done in my life.

As a little girl, my biggest curiosity was this - How does or would it feel to have a father? A father that lived in the home with you, raised you, and loved and cared for you as his daughter. What would that energy feel like? I often watched my friends with their fathers to see if they would satisfy my curiosity; however, my question remained. When I was a freshman in high school, my curiosity was at an all-time high. The reason - I went to live with my maternal grandmother for the school year, and she lived directly across the street from my biological father. He knew who I was, and I knew who he was. I lived there for almost a year. He never said a word to me. I watched him care for his wife and two other daughters every day. I understood at a young age that he only saw me as a little girl in the neighborhood, not as his little girl in the neighborhood. That was my reality, and I lived with it.

Years later, that experience would spark another question in me. What does it feel like to be a father?

As a parent, my curiosity was again at an all-time high. I often asked my husband, "How does it feel to be a father?" I would watch him with our daughter, hoping my curiosity would be filled. My husband would share his feelings and thoughts with me, which I was so grateful for because I knew our daughter would know firsthand the answer to my question.

I experienced a range of thoughts and feelings about not having a father as a child, which I'm sure you can imagine. Yet, in spite of these feelings, I always knew I would be alright without a father. How did I know? My great-grandmother told me, "Gal, you can't miss nothin' you never had!" Her words rang deep within me, and I've carried them until today.

As I got older, my curiosity continued to grow, and I knew my questions weren't going away. So, I began to ask my male friends two questions: "What does it feel like to be a father, and how are you doing as a father?" Momentarily, both questions gave them a pause, but to my surprise, they answered my questions and more!

I received many answers that helped me. I later recognized the answers were part of my healing process. The wisdom, transparency, and depth of their words caused me to feel grateful for my experiences and reality. I am thankful because my biological father's absence was part of a winning hand that God dealt me for my life. Yes, a winning hand! All the experiences, good and bad, have shaped me into the woman I am today. I am overwhelmed with joy at how God turned my curiosity into a beautiful healing.

One thing I know for sure is that everything in life is better when shared. So, I asked my male friends from all walks of life if they would join me by sharing their stories, experiences, feelings, and lessons with the world with the intent to heal, love and put great energy out into the earth. To my surprise, they said, "Yes!"

I believe it's our responsibility to give our children hope, leave a legacy they can be proud of and inspired by, and instill a curiosity that provokes magical growth.

No one has it all together or figured out; I certainly do not. So, the intent of *A Fatherless Curiosity* is to share our process of digging deeper, making mistakes, trying again, getting it right, winning, and continuing to grow personally by trusting God.

God has dealt us all a winning hand with the opportunity to live in freedom, to love, and the gift of being ourselves while doing it!

Thank you for taking this journey with us. Through the pages of this powerful anthology, I pray you will find experiences, systems, tools, and encouragement to apply forgiveness, love, and healing to overcome all.

Tyra

Serign Marong

Serign Marong was born in Las Cruces, NM, but grew up in Pullman, WA. His father is from The Gambia, and his mother's family is mainly Swedish. Pullman, where Washington State University (WSU) resides, is the quintessential college town. Most families either operate a farm or work for the university; Serign's was the latter.

Serign attended WSU, majored in biology/pre-med, and played football for the Cougs. Upon graduation, he worked for the university in anatomy and chemistry while applying for medical school. During this time, he met Visa, who would become his first wife. They moved to Seattle together when Serign started medical school at the University of Washington.

By the time he graduated, Visa and Serign were married and moved to Olympia, WA, for his family medicine residency. They had two boys by this time. However, life really changed when Visa passed away in March 2014.

After this tragedy, Serign struggled to get his life back on track and even quit medicine for a while. Through the grieving process, he moved to California, worked in a machine shop with his in-laws, and worked on a golf course. Also, through this process, he met his future wife, Michelle, and eventually returned to medicine. This led Serign to Tucson, AZ, where he has practiced family medicine for the past five years.

Serign and Michelle have a beautifully blended family of five kids, "yours, mine, and ours," where the youngest is two years old.

CHAPTER 1

A Journey Through Absence and Loss

Serign Marong, MD

My name is Serign Marong, and I am the father of five children (three biological) in a beautifully blended family. I consider being a father my most important responsibility that I have the privilege to improve upon every day. Two life-altering experiences have forged my perspective on this significant role. The first was growing up without my father, and the second was the death of my first wife.

My father is from The Gambia in West Africa. He came to the U.S. for high school and college, and it was in college that he met my mother. I was born in the States but lived most of my first year of life in The Gambia. Over the next few years, my mom and I lived in Washington until we lived in The Gambia again when I was around five years old.

I was young, but I remember a lot, like my pet baboon Manel, and my dad telling me to watch out for snakes as I walked through rice fields. I remember having elaborate escape routes planned in case wild boars chased me. Vultures circled our compound, and large monitor lizards snuck into our chicken coup and ate them all. Things were good, although we often visited family members who had no running water or electricity. I remember using a hole in the ground in the middle of the night with a lantern to go to the "bathroom," plus the open well you could fall into in the middle of the compound (yard). But everything changed when it was time for me to start school.

The original plan was to raise me in the U.S. for education, but when it came time for me to start, my father had a change of heart. My mom has mentioned this disagreement, but I don't remember much detail. Regardless if it was family or cultural pressure, the fact remains that we returned home alone, and my father chose to stay behind, leading to the beginning of my foundations on the ideal of fatherhood.

Since that separation, I have only seen the man twice. The first of those interactions was when I was eight years old when he came to visit. I remember him getting me a gift, a white and green scooter, which was pretty cool. It's funny, as I write this, riding scooters at the skate park is a favorite activity of my boys. But this visit was weird. I had forgotten and was a little scared of him. One day, watching Saturday morning cartoons, I behaved like a bratty kid, yelling for my mom to get up and make me some pancakes. I heard a deep voice calmly ask me to come down the hall. I will never forget the quiet, stern, African accent voice stating, "Do not yell for your mother like that." Maybe my mom would say differently, but I don't think I ever yelled like that again. Of course, I had times of misbehaving like any other kid, but that lesson of respect impacted me, even though he was gone just days later.

That was third grade when he visited, and I would not see him again for over 30 years. However, that did not bother me growing up. My mom did a wonderful job raising me, and I had a grandpa and an uncle who were close by and incredibly involved. I remember the ritual of wrestling my grandpa after Sunday dinners, baseball with my uncle, and golfing with both during the summer. My grandpa was pretty much at every single sporting event. Even later, when he had Parkinson's Disease and had a hard time with stadium stairs, he still came to my college football games. But I will not sell my mom short here. I remember her teaching me how to ride a bike, and the two of us frequently went to the family swim session at the pool in the summer. Dinner and movies were also a ritual. I remember playing catch with her in the backyard. One day I hit the Wiffle ball into our neighbor's yard. They had two big dogs who could get very excited. The neighbors weren't home, but we knew the dogs and thought it was ok to go in. In their excitement, they knocked me down, and I started screaming, which ended up with me getting bit in the leg, leading to an Emergency Room trip. Who picked me up and carried me out of that yard? My mom.

With my courageous single mom, plus my uncle and grandpa's involvement, I didn't notice any anger or sadness about my father's absence. But, of course, later in life, it became obvious that anger and a hole were developing inside me. I do, however, remember at a young age thinking that when I have kids, I will be the opposite of my father. I told myself that I will always be around. My kids will not need the male teacher like my mom thought I needed. But let me take a moment to recognize that my sixth-grade teacher, Mr. Jensen, is still a favorite. I told myself that any additional positive male role model, such as an uncle, grandpa, coach, or teacher, would just be a bonus and not a necessity for my future kids. So rather than having my father's actions and behaviors inspire me, the absence of those assets led to my motivation to be a good and present father.

This motivation to be a positive male role model started even before I had kids. In college, I became a Big Brother to two young Black kids who didn't have a father around. I played video games with them, rode bikes, did sports, took them to college basketball games, and more. This was the first time I even changed a diaper. I did not know what I was doing, which is quite comical when I look back. Many people thought they were my kids. Around this time is when some of the anger toward my father surfaced. That I had done more with these kids in a small amount of time than he ever had with me was a spark for this anger. I didn't realize it then, but because of his absence, I was driven to succeed, to prove that it did not affect me.

My first big success was in athletics. I was an all-around athlete in high school and played college football on a scholarship for Washington State University (Go Cougs!) The attention I got from that helped fill or perhaps helped cover up the hole inside me. This success fueled me for a long time. It made me feel I was worthy, yet I think deep down, I didn't truly feel worthy because I still could not understand how my father chose not to be a part of my life. What was wrong with me? Why did he not want me? I was a good player, but not a great one, and playing after college was not in my future. So, I set my sights on another lofty goal. I applied to medical school. It turns out it wasn't easy to do (go figure). I struggled to get in, which was a bit of a gut check I wasn't used to. But I made it, and my subconscious checked off another thing I achieved without him.

Even though becoming a doctor was a personal goal, I didn't realize until years later how much of that goal was conceived because of my father's absence. In my mind, if I could be a successful doctor, then my father's absence did not affect me. Clearly, he made a mistake in missing out on my life. Here I am, a big linebacker at a D1 school and now going to become a doctor. I was bigger, stronger, faster, and smarter than him, and I would never be one to abandon my kids.

My father and I have had little chance to discuss these feelings, man-to-man or father-to-son. As I write this, his health is not good, and he has some cognitive problems. But we did exchange words years ago, and I know he disagreed with my feeling of abandonment. Whether he had good reasons, or perhaps it was a cultural difference, it doesn't matter. In the end, I was still the little boy who didn't understand why his father didn't want to be with him. That feeling forged me into the man I am today, but before it made me strong, it almost destroyed me.

As I mentioned, I felt I was better than him because of all my success. I had done great things and had admirable goals going forward in life. But the origins of my goals were built on shame and fear. Although these foundations held me up for a long time, they were not firm foundations. When I struggled in medical school, those foundations began to shake. My wife, Visa, and I had our first son at the beginning of my family medicine residency. Overall, I was a good father, but I was living with shame and fear and was stuck in depression. Everything was a blur, and I was just going through the motions of life. Sure, I could completely blame things on the 80-hour workweek of a medical residency, but many times when I came home at night, I was not very present for my wife or the two boys we now had. Eventually, I learned to accept help. In fact, it was a lot of professional help. At first, needing help felt like a failure, but I know now that it takes courage to accept it. That is something I will make sure my kids know.

After receiving this help, life was looking good. I had completed my residency, and we were excited about our future. We discussed new cars, paying off bills, planning family trips, and planning a new medical career path. But on March 4, 2014, that all changed when my wife died suddenly and unexpectedly, leaving our two young boys and me. Ironically, she died of a blood clot in her lungs from birth control pills during a time we considered trying for a third child. As a result, those foundations I mentioned earlier began to crumble.

This sudden loss, this tragedy, was the next thing that shaped my view on fatherhood. After Visa died, I didn't know what to do. I took time off from my medical practice to figure out life. I tried grief therapy, but looking back, I just wanted to avoid the pain. I did not want to address it. I drank too much and used new relationships as a distraction from my pain. I moved out of our house because it was too painful, but when I moved into a new home, I ended up decorating it the way I thought Visa would have, anyway. I got rid of our old cars and bought the new one we had talked about getting. All the while I did these things, sometimes my boys were with me and other times with Visa's family. Just like the demands of residency gave some reason for my actions, my new disappointing behaviors were partially understandable given the situation. But the problem was those actions contradicted my values as a father.

While I struggled to define my new life as a single father, I did a lot of things to avoid the pain of grief, but what I did not do was focus on my boys. Sure, I played with them, laughed, bathed, and fed them. But much of the time, I was numb. Just like when I was depressed before, I was going through the motions of life. Now, considering this traumatic loss, can you blame me? No one really could. But people were almost too understanding and caretaking in a sense. My wife has a large Laotian family with five older sisters who were eager to fulfill their auntie roles, and there was no doubt that I needed the help. But too much responsibility was taken from me. I grew lazy and detached. I'm not blaming anyone, but with other people around who could take better care of my boys, I figured, why not? It makes me wonder. Did my father feel that way? Did he think it was best to let others take care of me?

The two years following Visa's death were a roller-coaster. Constant ups, downs, and curves I was not expecting. I went from suicidal to joining a new medical practice, quitting medicine, new relationships, drinking too much, moving to California, working in a machine shop with my brothers-in-law, and even doing valet at a golf course. Throughout this turmoil, my boys were mainly with their aunties. I was becoming a dad who was visiting them rather than raising them. As a result, I was absent and chose other things over them. Again, it's easy to justify some reasons, but the ironic sadness is that I was becoming my father.

At this point, my crumbling foundations were dust. They were nothing. I had to build new foundations for life, and they needed to be built on something solid rather than from fear, shame, or abandonment. Our boys were not quite two and four years old when their mom died. Now they were close to five and seven years old, and I had lost temporary custody of them because I could not get my life together. I was in a new relationship that I was desperately trying to hold on to, but again, I was doing it for the wrong reasons, so it did not last. So now, I had lost my wife, lost my kids, and lost a new relationship that was giving me some happiness. Two years prior, when my wife died, I thought about killing myself. Instead, I continued to exist but not live. In other words, a slow death. After this further loss, I finally accepted that I needed real help. On a side note, acceptance is listed as the final stage of grief.

The help I got was crucial, and I was ready for it this time. I did grief and trauma work. I took a parenting class to prove to my sister-in-law and the courts that I could care for my boys. It wasn't like a light bulb or lightning bolt experience that helped me turn the corner, but I started thinking about the legacy I would leave my boys. Back then and now, I still have some bitterness toward my dad, which is the unfortunate truth of his legacy to me.

I haven't mentioned the second time I saw him. It was the summer of 2019, and he was in the U.S. for medical care. For the longest time, I fantasized about meeting him and physically looking down on him. I didn't have the football frame I used to, but I was still a decent size guy. I don't think he even recognized me at first, and he seemed more overwhelmed than me. It was surreal. There was awkwardness, but no harsh words were expressed. The whole interaction was brief, but I'm very grateful it happened. Getting to meet him as a man and father gave me a little closure, plus he got to meet his grandsons (and my new wife). I still have a little bitterness, and I must carry that for now, and I am ok with that. But I do not want my boys to carry any bitterness for me. They had already lost their mother at an early age. They were home with her when she slumped down on the floor, clutching her chest and having trouble breathing. The older one remembers this. This is part of their story, and there is nothing I can do to change that. But what I can change is how they remember me. I can help them write new, wonderful chapters of their lives. If they can grow up, look back, and be proud of their dad, then I have done a good job.

Losing their mom is a huge part of our story, yet it is not the end of our story. I do not feel that we ever get over grief. It never completely resolves, but we learn to live with it. I learned to live with it by working on my internal happiness. Although my number one goal was to get my kids back after emerging from my dark hole of depression, the only way I could get them back was to be happy on my own. I had to do everything for myself and alone. Sure, it would sound great to say I did everything for them, but it had to be for me. I had to have this attitude to reach my ultimate goal: to be the father I never had.

From this tragedy comes triumph. I still don't like the saying that "everything happens for a reason." Don't tell me she is in a better place. But I like the idea of looking for the silver lining in a horrible situation. A book I read has a title that speaks to me. "A Grace Disguised," by Jerry Sittser, who also had a sudden tragic loss of family members. I have read this book a couple of times, and I will probably read it again. In the closing of his book, he talks about the positive changes that came from his tragedy. Before his wife's death, he "performed as a father," and after her death, he stated, "I am a father now, deep inside."

Truly realizing what it means to be a father is the unexpected, and maybe even undeserved, gift this tragedy has given me. I grew up without my father and have learned what that did to me. I cannot do that to my kids. But being physically present is not enough. Even though my mother did an amazing job as a single mom and made me the man I am today, looking back, I realize I needed more. I needed a dad to comfort me when I failed, to share his failures and successes with me, to tell lame jokes, to let me win playing one-on-one basketball or racing, and to give *a look* when I was out of line and disrespectful. I needed a dad to tell me it was ok to cry but also encourage me to be brave, to question the reasons for my goals but help me take the steps towards achieving them, a dad to model how to treat a woman and just people in general. And I needed a dad I could call in the middle of the night to ask for help or just say hi because I needed to hear his voice. These statements do not diminish my mom's pivotal role in raising me, nor do they lessen the victories of other single parents, but they are my motivations for being a father and a parent.

The absence of my father and losing my true self have taught me the father I want to be. But the teachings don't stop there. With the loss of my first wife and learning to live with grief, I have learned to be more present. The relationship I mentioned earlier ended; well, her name is Michelle. We are now married and have a two-year-old together. We have five kids total because Michelle brought two kids into the marriage. I am more present these days with all our kids. This awareness allows me to learn from them.

I remember when we told the kids we were moving in with Michelle and her kids. My oldest had immediate yet quiet, happy tears. At that moment, he realized the family we were about to become. Another story that sticks out was from a year before that moment when things really turned the corner. I was at the beach with my two boys, sitting in the sand, enjoying the sun, and watching them play in the shallow water. I was visiting them, and they hadn't been around me very much. While listening to them giggle and wrestle with each other, the younger one looked up and yelled at me. He said, "Hey Daddy…this is the best day ever!" It still gives me goosebumps and brings tears to my eyes, even as I write this years later. At that moment, none of the drama that had been happening mattered. That little guy was with his brother and his dad, and all was good. That is a moment I hold onto. Of course, not every day is a sunny day at the beach. But as long as I continue to live with a certain attitude and respect for the past, I have faith that my kids will write great chapters in their life stories.

One final thought about that uncle I mentioned earlier. He visited a couple of years ago, and we had a good chat. He is one of those guys that is sometimes short on words but has great things to say. I don't remember how the conversation started, but I was telling him about a dad I know who focuses more on golfing and trips with his buddies than he does on his kid's activities. My uncle said something to the effect of, it's not our time anymore. It is our children's time and their turn in this young life. Well, I have had my childhood, and it was a great one, despite my father's absence. It is now my responsibility and privilege to give my kids their chance at a great childhood, despite the tragedy they have experienced.

That is what fatherhood means to me.

Epilogue

I finished writing my chapter in May 2022. As I write this addition today, in December 2022, my father has now passed away. I had an idea that this day could be coming soon, as I knew his health was deteriorating. In fact, a month ago, I thought I should plan a trip soon to visit The Gambia while he was still alive.

The morning I heard the news, I had a couple of missed calls from my half-siblings and cousins in The Gambia. I immediately thought it would be bad news, but I felt prepared to hear it. After I got off the phone with my sister, I had immediate tears. I had been in the car, and when I got home, I ran in to hug my wife and started sobbing.

Why was I so sad about a man I barely knew? About a man who, in my eyes, chose not to be a part of my life? Even though I didn't know him, he was still a huge part of my life. As I said previously, his absence guided my idea of fatherhood just as much as if he had raised me.

I can honestly say I'm so grateful we got to meet a few years ago. I would feel a greater loss and confusion if that didn't happen. Things would feel unfinished, and I would have to work on that acceptance. However, I was able to get some closure in that brief meeting. I still wish I could have had a meaningful conversation with him, but there are numerous things in life we can't control.

So, after my initial emotion of hearing the news, it gave me immediate reflection on life and how precious time is. I know he regretted not having a relationship with me. That notion reminds me to be present for my boys today and not take anything for granted. My father lived into his 70s, but life is too short. It has taught me to be grateful for today and not settle for unacceptable situations.

I don't want to worry or focus much on the future. That causes anxiety. But I do want to look forward, with respect to what I do today. In other words, if I can picture myself years from now, looking at what I do today, and feeling content with those actions, then I should continue. If I can picture myself wanting to handle things differently, it is time to change. For example, I work a lot but could put in more clinic hours to make more money for my family. But that would come at the cost of taking away precious time I have with my kids that I can NEVER get back. Therefore, I'm happy with my hours and income.

Of course, everyone's situation is different, but the concept is the same. So ask yourself, whether you are a father, a mother, a grandparent, or some other significant role in a child's life, are you doing the things today that you will be content and proud of in the future?

Damarius Bilbo

Damarius Bilbo is the Head of Football for Klutch Sports Group, the powerhouse sports agency representing some of the biggest athletes across major professional sports. Previously Bilbo served as Director of Recruiting for Five Star Athlete Management, making his mark by helping them acquire and retain top talent and successfully transitioning college athletes into the NFL. In his first NFL Draft, Bilbo signed two first round selections, and over the course of six subsequent drafts, he signed 15 first round selections and secured over 40 clients. In 2013, Bilbo began his own agency, Revolution Sports Management, before joining Klutch in 2020.

A former High School National Player of the Year in football and MLB pitcher and outfielder prospect selected by the Milwaukee Brewers, Bilbo is a passionate athlete advocate and was honored with the Power 30 Under 30 Award in recognition of his outstanding work ethic and dedication to the community. Bilbo holds a B.S. in Management Information Technology and Industrial Design from the Georgia Institute of Technology and is currently based in Atlanta.

CHAPTER 2

What Could Have Been…

Damarius Bilbo

My nickname from my family has always been "Man." At the time, I understandably didn't see it as a personality thing but more as a "southern thing." Maybe it was because I was a big baby at birth or because I had a very adult-like demeanor, even at a young age. My mother, Deborah, later told me it was through a conversation we had that I told her, "I will now be the man of the house." That's how I got the nickname "Man."

Being raised in the south by a single mother always seemed normal to me. I never had an affectionate memory of my father, only unenthusiastic stories from my grandmother and other family members, along with damaging memories. Maybe I was too young to recollect, or maybe I subconsciously blocked the remembrances out, but that portion of my life is mainly a blur. I knew that my parents dated for a few years when my younger brother and I were born; however, my early childhood was filled with countless disappointments and shattered hopes from a nonexistent father. As we became old enough to appreciate household roles, I never really felt that I was missing anything since there wasn't a man in the house. This was primarily because my mother worked extremely hard and sacrificed much of herself to ensure all the needs were met. Her saying was always, "The Lord is your father, and he just loaned you to me while you're here on earth." I never fully understood what this meant as a child because I never saw God's face. Ironically, I rarely saw my real father's face either. I simply took my mother's words as her way of telling us not to look towards a man to lead and aid us with figuring out this world and its problems because, as humans, we are all flawed and should serve a perfect God. Instead of constantly comforting us and making excuses after the shattered hopes of having a relationship with our biological father, teaching us about a more dependable God would have lasting benefits. To that point, my mother never spoke poorly about my father or his poor choices; she simply dealt with the circumstances of his absence and made sure to provide us with an understanding of who we were with or without him... God's children.

Growing up, there was never really a familiar example of fatherhood for me. My grandfather, who I really admired and saw as an exceptional man, was aged, and his health had declined by the time I was old enough to inquire about my early years with my father and his own father. My mom and aunts used to tell me stories about how he would walk to church and race them outside for hours. When he and my grandmother divorced, he still provided and took care of her other kids as his own. I had uncles that were solid men and providers for their children, but circumstances in the relationships with their kids' mothers didn't allow those moments to be consistent enough for the bonds to mature as they should. Very few of my childhood friends had fathers around, and if they were, they didn't seem to be that involved with their kids, mainly because they were too busy with work and trying to support the household. Where I was raised in south Mississippi, a strong single mother seemed to be the head of the household in most black family structures. Because of this, I always knew that regardless of the circumstance I was experiencing, I wanted to break the cycle of fatherlessness within my family.

My mother was the one who directed me toward sports. I was really into drawing and art, which kept me indoors and out of trouble, but she understood that the responsibilities and roles that both parents should be splitting were now squarely on her shoulders. For her, that meant me getting outside of the house and developing a personality and relationships to help me become a "man." In the south, there were plenty of easy ways to get into trouble. Rather than allowing me to roam the streets and eventually find trouble, she knew that becoming an athlete would be a way for me to be productive and learn the structure I was missing from a man. I wasn't a loud kid or shy, just somewhere in between. I listened more than I spoke, but never really hearing or receiving advice from a man at first seemed odd. I heard my friends' fathers shout out commands which always seemed to upset them, so if having a coach was anything like that, it wasn't something I was looking forward to.

All my childhood and teenage years were spent in sports, so I saw different expressions and systems of fatherhood through coaches and fathers around the sport. Coaches have always played the biggest role as father figures in my life. They provided the structure and discipline that all young boys needed growing up. I respected them because they gave me knowledge and respect, but most importantly, they taught me accountability and the importance of "doing what you say you will do." These lessons stayed with me throughout my youth. All of my coaches had different personalities, approaches, and outlooks on life, but they all were similar in their beliefs in what defined a man and how you should conduct and carry yourself as one. The lessons I learned from every single coach have stayed with me and are some that I implement throughout my journey as a father.

As a player seeing the fathers of my teammates come around, I saw things that always intrigued me and sometimes made me ask myself, "Am I really missing anything by not having my father around?" There were relationships where some fathers were clearly there to support their sons. But sometimes, wanting them to be so successful in the sport, they applied unnecessary pressure on their kids, making them frustrated and uncomfortable, which eventually hurt their relationship. There were fathers who were never there because they worked so many hours; they were too tired and overwhelmed to attend certain events, which disappointed the child and also ended up tarnishing the relationship. Constantly seeing these scenarios perplexed me because my dad was absent. I didn't understand or have emotions toward those father-son factors, and at times I honestly felt relieved and somewhat lucky. Observing these scenarios left me confused. Without those personal experiences, I didn't fully understand or develop the many emotions in the relationship dynamics between a father and his children.

I first met my father around the age of 11 and over the phone again during my senior year of high school. My mother's friend, who I referred to as my godmother, who lived in New Orleans, called my mother and said that our father wanted to see my brother and me. My mom didn't really talk to us about it, but she agreed to take us on the short trip to see him. All we knew was, "Get in the car. We are headed to New Orleans," which was where he lived at the time. Once there, my brother and I walked the city with him (at the time, my brother was 9), and all I remember him doing was constantly accusing my mother and blaming her for him not having a relationship with us. There seemed to be no accountability or explanation as to why he, as our father, decided that he could exit our lives and leave our mother with all the obligations of raising two men that he helped bring into this world. My brother was younger and seemed a bit more excited about his promises of building a relationship with us, but I didn't trust that someone who so easily went away would suddenly be strong enough to come back and stay. We ended the day with him giving me a handful of money, which I gave to my brother, and that was it. I guess in his eyes, one day full of open promises and fun could make up for years of neglect. The entire ride home, my brother just talked about how cool "Dad" was and how excited he was to know he wanted to see us, and when was the next time we would get together. I had a weird feeling that this would be the first and last time we saw him, so I protected my brother's emotions, ensuring he didn't suffer from the disappointments this encounter would bring. After this encounter with our father, I began to experience more anger. I was around the age of

12 or 13 when I started to question why my father didn't stay around. Were we not good enough for him? Was there something that he struggled with that we didn't know about that led him to exit his responsibilities as provider and "head of household?" Why did we even have to meet this guy only to have him come in and disrupt what, in my mind, had been a smooth upbringing by an amazing woman?

The next time I "heard" from my father was years later, close to the end of my senior year of high school. As I grew older and became more accomplished in athletics, I received numerous compliments, accolades, and scholarships from men that control universities across the nation. I had just led my football team to the 5A state championship title, and the year before, in baseball, I helped lead the team to the state championship game, which we ended up losing. I was one of the country's top two sports prospects, so I received calls from many universities and a ton of pro scouts. Even during those moments, I still questioned why my father wasn't present and why I was left to figure so much out on my own, which often left me frustrated. My mother knew nothing about the process but attempted to learn on the fly, which was hilarious to experience. Seeing her sit through meetings, sometimes dozing off or answering phone calls and saying, "He's not here" and "This isn't his mother," merely because we both were over the recruiting process. It was eventful, to say the least.

On a random weeknight, I received a call from someone I thought to be a coach or scout attempting to persuade me to go pro in baseball and pass on going to college. He ended the conversation by confessing that he was my father and started to give details that only a father would know. I asked my mom to pick up the phone, and he answered a few of her questions, which confirmed that he was who he said he was. The phone call served as a reminder that he was well aware of "how" to contact us; he just didn't feel the need to ever "want" to. For years, this experience gave me a "what could have been" complex because from that moment on, I started to replay almost every moment that meant something in my life and thought about what could have been if he were present.

I never spoke to him again until we became friends on Facebook years later. That has been the extent of our relationship. No dinners, no extensive phone calls or texts, no holidays or milestones or memories. Seeing his "son" getting drafted in baseball, receiving full scholarship offers and playing college football, graduating from college and having an opportunity to play pro sports, and even becoming a grandfather, are all things that he forfeited. I never understood the psychology of a man who could help create a child, leave a household, and just continue with life as if a part of him never existed. I often felt that even if everything he said about his relationship with our mother was true years before, there was no barrier placed on his involvement in our lives. So who is really to blame for what he missed out on?

All that I didn't experience or have while growing up is exactly why I wanted to be a father, to show that despite my lack of models, I could raise a fruitful child who exemplified love and trust in relationships. I didn't want just to be present or provide support but to be impactful and have an eventful experience with my children. When I became a father, it became more of a *what not to do and what did you see on TV* approach because I didn't have many positive male examples. I've heard from many black men I know that most of the father figures we saw were on TV. Fred Sanford from *Sanford and Son*, Uncle Phil from the *Fresh Prince,* Carl Winslow from *Family Matters,* and Bill Cosby from *The Cosby Show* were our models. These TV fathers struggled with family issues, but they were present and impacted their children's lives by staying and teaching lessons that carried them through life. Even though it was television, it provided a real script for my life and lessons as a father.

My only son, Aiden, was born when I was 25. His mother and I dated a few years and were both starting our professional careers. She never really expressed the desire to be a parent, but she had all the qualities to be an amazing mother. When she discovered that she was pregnant while working out of the country, we both had to plan accordingly because life would forever be changed. I had to immediately learn that fathering was more than simply providing food, clothing, and shelter for a child while letting the mother who carried them take care of the rest. I was always fairly good with time management and didn't have a selfish personality, which I attributed to sports. I learned that fatherhood meant giving time and being selfless in every act and action that presents itself as it pertains to your child. I wanted to be fully engaged in his development from day one and provide him with continued reassurance of my love and devotion because, in the end, it wasn't his choice to enter this world. Unlike sports, there was no playbook for raising Aiden, my firstborn, and a life I was now responsible for. I knew from day one that I didn't want to leave him with disappointments because of my failure to be present. I had so many doubts because I had never practiced for this moment. As an athlete, you regularly have a game plan you rehearse and ask questions about before you go out to perform. Becoming a father was unknown and unrehearsed, and I was terrified. I blamed my father for not being nearby and leaving me to figure this out again. Some moments before his birth were filled with joy and others with depressed states, simply because I felt unqualified and untrained on how to be a man for another human being.

In the days and weeks leading up to his birth, I found myself calling my mom countless times throughout the day for reassurance. She would always provide me with spiritual counsel first, then give me words of encouragement like, "Just be the father to him that you never had. Treat him the way you would've wanted your dad to treat you. Give him everything you didn't have." Taking my mother's advice, the first thing I prepared when he was born was I created an email address for him. I began sending him messages and memories explaining moments in his life that he perhaps wouldn't remember as he got older. I did this because I recalled the heartache that overcame me when asking my mom for pictures of me as a baby, and she only had one because my father didn't allow them. I wanted my son to remember everything about his childhood, but more importantly, about our relationship. When he was born, his mother and I were both first-time parents, and the emotions began. I was still chasing the football dream at the time but still made it to Alaska to be there for his birth. That day was such an unexplainable feeling, and at that moment, I knew it was real. I had a choice to make, and there was no hesitation in my mind that he would never have to live without me in his life. For the first few months, he had to stay in Alaska with his mother until she was able to travel back to Atlanta with him. Those weeks were the worst because I could not bond with him. Although she assured me that I wasn't missing anything but sleep and feeding, I didn't want to start our relationship with me not being nearby.

Aiden is now 14 years old, and I have been extremely active in his life and development as a young man and teenager. I sometimes get frustrated with him because there are moments I feel he may take for granted having an active father in his life. I've made the mistake of saying things out of frustration in the moments when he doesn't take advantage of having me available to communicate with and be present daily. He will never have to understand what it feels like to reach puberty or even attend big games without someone (his father) there to lean on for emotional support and advice. He won't have to sleep at night wondering if the person who helped bring him into this world even cares if he is alive. These are constant questions that have presented themselves throughout my journey.

My son Aiden is now a proud big brother to my daughter Camryn, 3 years old. Because of their age gap, I was able to absorb more parenting experience by the time she arrived. Raising Aiden wasn't difficult at all because he was an extremely "chill" baby and child. We developed routines and memories that he still remembers to this day. He's always had a natural "cool" about himself and just goes with the flow. He is an exceptionally smart student-athlete, and although I don't push him toward sports, I give him the resources while letting him find his passion in whatever life he chooses. I would be lying if I didn't admit that every day is tough trying to raise a boy into a teenager and eventually a man. The world's much more complicated than it was while I was growing up. Although I didn't have a father in my life or strong examples of one, there weren't many distractions that influenced the information I was getting from my mother and coaches. Today, so much access is at a child's fingertips, such as social media, and I constantly pray that he relies on me for information instead of other methods.

I still contribute photos and videos to Aiden's email while also maintaining one for my daughter. Technology allows so many memories to be shared over time, and I want to make sure both know that we made them our priorities. My patience level has grown a bit, especially now that I have a daughter. Camryn is a living baby doll with the energy of two kids. There is a vast emotional difference between raising a male and a female, and I am thankful that the Lord has allowed me to raise two healthy children. I take nothing for granted, and every day is a great day when I'm able to be present as a parent and provider. I'll be the first to admit that there is real trauma going from fatherless to fatherhood, but I make sure to incorporate what my mother told me years ago. "Just be the dad that you wanted." The greatest lesson that I have learned from my son is *just listen.* Allow him to process his emotions and find the words to express how he is feeling. Have faith and trust that he believes in our relationship enough to come to me if there is ever a problem or situation that he needs guidance on.

I often tell individuals who have lost a father to appreciate the opportunities they had to make memories because my father is currently alive, yet I have very few memories, good or bad. So even in death, you have more of them to carry you through than I ever had with mine, who is still full of life. I say this to say that I only hope that whenever I leave my children's lives that my exit would only increase their love for me and encourage how they parent their children because of how I lived my life with and for them. No day is perfect, but being consistent and allowing them to see the effort and attention are all valuable. I've learned that you don't have to have examples of how to be a father. You only need to love yourself enough to love and grow with your children. I now understand my mother's "borrowed time" theory, as it refers to our relationship as parents and with God. There have been countless hours of prayer that while I am their father here on earth, He provides me with everything I require to support them in becoming individuals that reflect His goodness and grace in our lives. There is certainly no playbook on fatherhood, but you must be in and stay in the game to get it right. I know deep down that my children will never have to grow up wondering "what could have been" when it comes to our relationships.

Therome James

A powerful, positive, larger-than-life force of personality, Therome James brings a unique brand of engagement and wholeness to his classroom daily. Therome is a master at teaching others to enjoy the greater version of themselves and creating the love of Physical Science which he teaches!

Therome is a Certified Teacher, coach, mentor, speaker, and seminar presenter. Therome received his teaching certification from the East Central University, Ada, Oklahoma.

Therome is presently teaching 8th-grade Physical Science in Kennesaw, Georgia at Awtrey Middle School, where he specializes in changing the mindset of students about the subject of science. He also has a mentoring program, Young Men of Awtrey (YWA), for boys in grades six through eight. Therome also coaches married couples with his wife, Tyra. He is a master at teaching others to learn, create, and implement a positive atmosphere in their classroom. Therome has had countless opportunities to teach this to the masses, including Perkins Local Schools and Townsend Community School in northeast Ohio, and Cobb County Schools in Georgia, during professional development programs.

Therome has been an educator for 38 years. In addition to his current teaching position at Awtrey Middle School, Therome serves on two boards, Swift Cantrell Foundation and Youth Education and Sports, both non-profit organizations in Kennesaw, Georgia.

Therome was a former co-host of the 1490 AM radio show, "Relationships," where he gave coaching advice to listeners live on the air.

Therome has always been active in his community. From 2010 through 2014, he created the Agape Love Summer Basketball League for boys in grades five through eight in Sandusky, Ohio. The league had over 200 players from the surrounding area. In 2010, he received the "Man of the Year" award for exemplary service to the community. In 2012, Therome collaborated with T.O.P.S. INC (Training on Prevention Services) and was named Co-City Leader for the youth tutoring program for the city of Sandusky. In 2014, he received an award as the top Minority Teacher in Ohio from CNN news. In the 2017-2018 school year, he was Cobb County Teacher of the Year. He was also nominated as one of the top five teachers 2022-2023. He is currently writing his first book entitled "A Fatherless Curiosity."

Therome is the husband of Tyra James for 29 years, and together they have a 27-year-old daughter Logan James. He is most grateful for the gift that God has given him to relate, inspire, and empower others.

CHAPTER 3

From The Crib to The Stage

Therome "TJ" James

Adad should love, show kindness, and be so in tune with his children that he often knows what is on their minds even before talking with them. He listens, suggests, and defends. But that was not my reality. I had nothing close to that growing up. Let me begin by setting the stage for you about my childhood. I had a dad in my life. He was a great provider for the family financially, but he gave nothing emotionally to me. My dad was a functioning alcoholic. He drank every day that I can remember as a young child.

He was also verbally abusive to me and physically and verbally abusive to my mother. I cannot recall a weekend when there was not something disturbing taking place in our home because of my dad's drinking. We would have to sleep with our clothes on at night just in case he came home after being at the bar and started putting his hands on my mother and putting us out no matter the hour or the season - even with the weather in Ohio ranging anywhere from 100° F to minus 5° F.

I was the oldest boy in the house, so I received most of the verbal abuse and my mother received all the verbal and physical abuse. I have three other siblings — an older sister, a younger sister, and a younger brother. Everything changed one winter night when my mother said enough is enough. She said she was going to be killed or kill him that night. At that moment, I had to say something. I was only 12 years old, and I told my dad to stop putting his hands on my mother with tears coming down my face, and he did. We left the next day to stay with my grandmother until my parents got a divorce. This all happened during the most influential time in childhood, my middle school years.

I didn't realize until later in my life how all this abuse affected me as a man. After having real-life conversations with my mother and my siblings, I discovered I had blocked my middle school years from my mind. Experiencing an upbringing like that was tough, mainly because I tried not to let anyone know how tough it was to sleep at night.

Even with all that dysfunction in my upbringing, I could not wait to be a dad. May 30, 1995, was one of the happiest days of my life, besides the day I married Tyra, my best friend, soulmate, and the love of my life. I remember that moment like it was yesterday. I was at the hospital at 4:00 p.m., repeating every word the doctor stated during the delivery of my daughter, Logan. At 5:00 p.m. that day, I walked into the hospital nursery, and every emotion possible entered my body. From that moment, I vowed to be present, loving, listening, suggesting, and defending during every stage of her life, from the crib to the stage.

In the Crib

This is where fatherhood began for me. I would spend every moment I could in Logan's room in her crib. Please understand that I am 6 foot, 2 inches, 225 pounds, and I would sit inside her crib singing every baby song to her while playing with the pretty things my wife had placed in her crib. I would video every moment we shared, even when she was asleep. Crazy right? I wanted every moment of her development on video. Logan would roll over and give me a pretty smile into the camera. She enjoyed playing peek-a-boo with me. Tyra would walk into the room and see me in her crib and say, "Really T." I wanted her always to know that I would be there when she went to sleep and when she woke up every day of her life, and it started at that point in her life. When she cried, I could not let that happen for an extended period for a reason.

Crawl Before You Walk

As a man raised mostly by his mom, as I explained earlier, being a father was never taught to me. I had to figure out many things on the fly. I did not have a dad who shared or gave me advice on how to invest in your child's life because he was not that type of father. My parents divorced when I was in the 8th grade. From that point on, I blocked most of my middle school experiences out of my memory. We did not have counselors that would help a young brother like myself deal with the separation from not having a father in the house. We always had food on the table and clothes on our backs, but until I reached age 32, there were no conversations about life with my dad. When I say I had to crawl before I could walk, I mean that. What's awesome about my relationship with my dad today is that I forgave him, we reconciled our relationship, and we talk every other day. I can ask him for advice, and he is always willing to share it. My teachable moment for any child or adult who has experienced a tough childhood with a parent is this - It is okay to have a conversation with your parent later when you are both willing to listen with an open heart and a forgiving mindset.

My mindset in raising Logan with my wife Tyra was to always be present and available at any cost, and that was exactly what I did from the beginning. Logan crawled backward before she walked forward. I believe I also did, as her father. Raising a child was a dream of mine. I wanted five kids at first. I am a true kid at heart, and I enjoy being around kids.

Back to the fact I had to crawl before I could walk. Tyra was going out of town for the weekend for the very first time since we had Logan. She was 3 years old. My wife would leave me detailed instructions on how I should take care of the house and Logan. The first day was so awesome. Logan and I would practice riding her bike in the grass, so we played outside all day. I made what I thought was Logan's favorite dish for breakfast, lunch, and dinner - waffles and turkey bacon. Everything was going so well until I got Logan's hair wet while giving her a bath. If you know anything about an African American girl's hair, you do NOT get it wet. So, I had to figure something out because we had to pick her mom up from the airport that evening. Can I just say with all honesty when we arrived at the airport on that warm sunny day, my beautiful daughter had on a Marvin Gaye knit hat and tears in her eyes. It was nothing nice.

The ride home was quiet on my end. Like any man, I thought I had the skills to put Logan's hair in a cute ponytail. It was not as easy as it looked when her mother did her hair. So, when I say I had to crawl before I could walk as a father, I meant that in every sense of the word. From that point on, I had a cosmetologist on call whenever Tyra went out of town. I would like to say to all new fathers, if you do not have the skills to do something even as simple as combing your daughter's hair, ask for help. That day was a true crawl-before-you-walk experience.

Life-Changing Day

This would have to be one of the scariest days for me as a father. Logan and I were shopping for her mom's birthday gift at Macy's in the Sandusky Mall. Logan and I would always play hide-and-seek at home at least once a day from age three to seven. Logan was getting good at keeping quiet, even when I was close to catching her. On this day, she did her best work. I could not find her for at least 30 minutes or more. I had the store call her name on the intercom system, but she did not respond. My fear was someone had kidnapped my daughter. My next thought was, how could I call home and tell Tyra I could not find our daughter? When I say scary, I mean it. After searching through every clothing rack in the store, I found Logan sitting inside a rack of Ann Taylor dresses with a pretty smile, and she said, "Daddy, I got you so good this time!" I hugged her so hard at that moment, and I could not help but remember that when she was born, I promised always to be present. I held her hand the rest of that day, and I said to her, "Logan, we can only play hide-and-seek at home." We still had not shared that story with her mom until now.

Quality Time

When raising a child, a father needs to be available to hear and see his child's struggles and successes. I would spend at least 15 to 20 minutes in Logan's room lying across her bed, asking about her day and how things are going in her life without interrupting or judging, from birth to the present day. I must be honest, when she reached high school she would say, "Mom, Dad is in my room again," but that never stopped me from checking in on her. As a father, I have learned that if you ask the right question, they will forget you are even there. Certainly, there are stages as a father where you need to know when to step back and when to step in. If you do not have that relationship with your child established early on, it will be tough in the later years to just start coming into their room to develop quality time. Remember, you must crawl before you can walk. For me, some of my best times were the talks in Logan's room and driving to and from school with her every day.

Walking up the Stairs

As I transitioned into fatherhood, I was blessed to be in the same building with Logan throughout her middle school years. I was her teacher for the first two years, and I was just her dad in the building the last year. Just before she began middle school, we sat down at the table to have our normal family meeting. On this day, we discussed what middle school should look like for Logan. At the school she would attend, teachers have the option to instruct their child if both parents and the child agree. Logan had total control at 12 years old to make the final decision. Her first thought was no, she would rather have a different teacher in science. So, we agreed because we wanted her to know we would support any decision she made. As her dad and as a teacher, she was entering what is often the most challenging three years of a child's life, with me hoping and praying she would feel confident enough in me to help her "walk up the stairs."

Logan's first response was not to have me as her teacher, but later that night, after talking with her friends on the phone, she came back and stated all her friends said, "If I could have Mr. James as my teacher, I would definitely choose him." As a father, it felt so good to know that my work in the classroom helped to create a bond with my daughter that I will never forget. We practiced at home for weeks before school started, with her calling me Mr. James. My teachable moment as her dad and teacher was when Logan said, "You never call on me in class to read or answer questions like all the other students." I was totally unaware I had done that, so from that point forward, I made sure I acknowledged her like all the other students in the room. I committed to not treating her differently than any other student in the class. We never discussed her behavior in my class at home. Even after she received her first detention in middle school from me for excessive talking. I thought for sure she would come home, and the first thing she would say to her mom at the dinner table would be, "Dad gave me a detention." She never mentioned a word. One of my greatest memories was when we created a secret handshake that we would do every day before school started.

When I said I would be present from the crib to the stage, I was. I watched my little girl transition into a beautiful, intelligent young lady right before my eyes. By the time 8th grade came, as a family, we all agreed she needed another teacher for science. Most of the students in the building had forgotten she was my daughter because she had called me Mr. James for two years. At home, we still had our quality time moments in her room, but the conversations were different because we never discussed school, instead it was mostly sports and friends.

A father plays a significant role in a child's growth during the middle school stages. Talking with Logan about life on the way home from school was such a blessing for me. Not every ride home was pleasant. In middle school, there are words that popped into my mind, like "I know it all." I had to learn as a father to let my daughter experience some things for herself because experience is sometimes the best teacher.

Her middle school upbringing differed from mine. I went to an all-Black school, and Logan was one of only five Black students in her school. As her father, I often wanted to eliminate some challenges of middle school from her life, but I could not be everywhere at every moment. I would often tell Logan that someone is always watching you, so make sure you make smart decisions. We would always have conversations about how people should address her by her name only, and no other way would be acceptable. We would remind her she had a voice and to use it when needed for expression, protection, or reflection.

A Missed Step

This was the second scariest moment in my time as a father. I made some poor decisions as a husband. I was unfaithful to my wife, Tyra, and this affected our home environment. We separated for four months; Logan was about 5 years old. I did not recognize at the time that I was leaving my daughter with the same memories I had in middle school. As I stated earlier, my parents divorced when I was in the 8th grade, and I was getting ready to give my daughter that same memory if I did not get back on that step and walk up the right way. Being a father involves far more than being a provider. We need to be invested in every aspect of being a father, husband, dad, coach, supporter, and cheerleader. I had to look in the mirror and do what I asked my daughter to do, make a smart decision because people are always watching, especially God. I could not see how selfish I was at that moment in my life. My behavior and actions affected my whole family in many ways, and I had chosen not to see it.

Fatherhood has such a powerful feeling behind it. The word hood means you are not alone. So often, as men, we try to handle life issues on our own because we are too prideful to ask for help. I had to be vulnerable, tell the truth about what I was doing, and not blame anyone but myself for my behavior. For me, the most challenging aspect of growth as a father was taking total ownership of my actions.

How could I expect my child to respect me and my decisions about her life if I could not lead by example? Remember, children do what we do, not what we say.

Tyra and I were separated for about four months the first time and one year the second time. During those periods of separation, I tried to always be available and present in Logan's life, despite not being at home with her every night. I would take her to school every morning. We would continue to act as if I still lived in the house with her. During those times, I had to evaluate and focus my intentions on how I should look, as a husband to my wife and as a father to our daughter. With Tyra's forgiveness, love, and support, we survived me missing a step on the stair climb toward high school with our daughter. As I mentioned earlier, everyone in the family was affected by my missed step, which meant I also needed to ask for Logan's forgiveness. And I did just that. Truth and humility of character are not only to be taught to our children through words but even more so by the actions we live in front of them. While separated, I remember these words my wife said to me, "T, is this the best you can do?" Her question helped me to realize that I could and should do better. It was the wake-up call that I needed. I knew in my heart that I had so much more to offer, and I desired to do the work to bring my family together again. I wanted to raise my daughter in our home, together with her mother. I realized I had to do some hard self-evaluation. I did not want to do it because I knew it would be tough. Let me keep it real, looking at yourself is not easy. And it is not for the faint of heart. In fact, it was downright painful. For me, pride got in the way, and I had the tendency to do anything and everything but search deep within myself. Honestly, I did not like who I was, and that was tough. But I knew to become the man I needed to be for our marriage to survive and thrive and to get my family back, I simply had to do the work. I did not do it alone. I had help from Pastors and my mother, all of whom were straightforward and honest with me. They spared me nothing, and I am still thankful for that today. After a year of self-work, I was eventually mature enough to have the conversation that was needed with my wife to bring a committed version of myself to our family. We came back together with restoration on our minds, and we have not looked back. My teachable moment — if it is a problem for one, it is a problem for the family. We agreed I would be the example of a loving and committed husband and father for my daughter from that day forward. We also agreed that I would be the first to buy flowers, diamonds, go on a date, and movies and give Logan the type of experiences she should expect to look forward to.

Still Present Between Steps

We pulled up to the high school for the first time; we did our prayer and our secret handshake, and she got out of the truck and never turned around. I pulled over and called my wife, crying because this would be my very first experience of not seeing Logan throughout the day. As a father, we believe we have given our children enough advice, expectations, and moral character to be successful in life. I watched her behavior around me in the middle school environment, but now I was concerned about not being able to be present during high school. I looked forward to taking her home each night after school to have our quality time conversations about her day.

I was still coaching high school basketball in her first two years of high school. For the last two years, we agreed as a family that I would focus on being a father, and I did. Logan played volleyball, and I wanted to be present at every game, so I was the announcer at all home games. At first, she did not want me to do it because she thought it would be embarrassing. But I gave all the girls nicknames during the introductions at the first game. They loved it, and at that point, she was all in.

As a father, there is nothing like watching your child grow and develop right before you. Fathers, try your best to be present with your children at every activity and in every conceivable way possible as they transition through life.

Holding Onto the Rail

As I walked up to the stage, I had to hold on to the rail tightly. Let me explain. Logan attended an all-White high school. There were about 20 total minority students in her high school. Remember, at the beginning of my chapter, I stated a father should also be a defender of their child. If anyone really knows me, they will say I have a good relationship with everyone and I am mild-mannered.

Like most parents, we want the best for our children, and we believe they deserve the same opportunities as everyone else. One night, Logan had her last away match as a senior on the volleyball team. The coach decided not to play her in the first two sets. Mind you, she was the starting outside or middle hitter all year. We lost the first two sets, and all the parents were yelling to put Logan in the game. The coach just looked at the parents and continued to coach the way he wanted. After losing the two sets, he then put Logan in the game, and they won the next two sets to go into the fifth set. The coach then decided not to play her again, and they lost the match. Afterward, my daughter was crying so hard about the situation, and I, as her father and defender, asked the coach a simple question. What was the reason behind playing her in the two sets after losing the first two and then not playing her to win the match? His response was, "I am the coach, and I make all the decisions. That is all I need to say to you." At that point, I lost all my patience, morals, and my ability to stay in character. I grabbed the coach by the neck and pushed him up against the mat on the gym wall while pushing his wife away from me. I told him he mistreated my daughter this night, and all the parents in the gym noticed he would rather lose a match than play one of his best players because she was Black. After several parents calmed me down and said to me, "TJ, it is not worth it," I released my hands from around his neck and left the gym.

That next Monday, I was called into the athletic department office to discuss the situation. Because I was a teacher in that school system, there could be some consequences. After spending several hours with the athletics director and Logan's coach, we agreed not to take the matter any further, but I made it clear to both that this should never happen to another player again. I also reminded them that this same situation could happen to them as fathers one day, and I hope they will remember how this matter was handled. My teachable moment as a father — I could have waited to calm down and scheduled a meeting with the athletic director and coach that next week to discuss the situation and not embarrass my daughter and ruin our family name. Yes, I had to hold on to the rail extra tight to make it up to the stage in that moment of fatherhood.

On The Stage

This was my proudest moment as a father. In our school system, if you are a teacher, you can give your child their high school diploma during graduation. Logan and I practiced our secret handshake for a few minutes that morning, and when they called her name, "Logan James," there I was on stage, and we did our famous secret handshake in front of thousands of students and parents, and the crowd went crazy. During that moment, I experienced every emotion a parent could have. I believed I had done everything possible to be the father I was called to be to my daughter. Just as I vowed when she was born, I was present from the crib to the stage.

William Logan

Born and raised in Lexington, Kentucky, William was an only child and grew up with both parents in his home. Since most of his friends (and foes) had siblings, William used comedy to fit in and to keep from getting "beat down" in the neighborhood. He attended the University of Kentucky and in the mid-80s, was part of a group that started WTLA, a cable radio station in Lexington. He was an on-air DJ for nearly four years. Through his years with the radio station, he honed his comedic skills, which led to an opportunity to open for the R&B group Midnight Star. He became the opening act and house comic for a local comedy club when comedy was booming. He had the pleasure of opening for such comedians as Steve Harvey and J. Anthony Brown. He also met the late B.B. King.

In the late 80s, William began selling office equipment and moved to Atlanta with his job. Still dabbling in stand-up when he arrived in Atlanta, William met the lady who would become his wife and had to decide - get married or continue stand-up (according to William, there was no way he could have done both). He chose marriage and has never looked back. When his twin sons were in high school playing baseball, an announcer for the games was needed, and another career began for William. Because of his love for the microphone, William became the PA announcer for high school baseball and basketball (and some college softball) for about ten years until the pandemic hit.

William is now retired and works as a ranger for a local golf course.

Facebook -William Logan

Twitter -chillewill

CHAPTER 4

It's a Mother Being a Father

William Logan

"It is easier to build strong children than to repair broken men."

~ Frederick Douglass

When my wife was pregnant, I was told there is no pamphlet, handout, or manual for fatherhood. When our children were born, I learned at the same time they did. As I looked into their faces, I learned what makes them smile, laugh, and cry. It's a journey that continues for the rest of your lives.

There are many ways to raise a child, but no matter how a child is raised, parents learn one thing very early. You will do anything for them. No matter where they are, what time it is, or what they have done, you will be there.

Yeah.

These are lessons that fathers must learn, but real learning starts when you are a child (ala Frederick Douglass).

I had both parents in my home when I was growing up. I got into some trouble (being an only child, trouble kind of follows you.) Not that I was a bad kid, but when you're the only child in the house, it always looks like you're the guilty one.

Disciplining by your parents (especially your father) lays the groundwork for what you see as discipline and love in your life. It becomes your litmus test for how you deal with all people, and you learn to accept it and roll with it. It becomes part of your personality.

I didn't realize there were different approaches to being a father until I was on a trip with my best friend in college.

Most of the fathers (if they were there) of my boys I hung around with growing up were in the same mold as my father. They worked hard, possibly had two jobs, and spent a lot of time on "the hill" at the package store (their meeting place to sit in the lot, drink, and talk shit). My father maintained everything in the house. If it broke, he could fix it.

Now when we went to my friend's hometown, and his father greeted him with a hug and a kiss on the cheek, I was floored! My first thought was, "OH HELLS NO!!!! That would never happen in my house." My father was an excellent provider and one of the most talented men I have known. He could rewire a house, then turn around and draw you a portrait. But emotionally, he was distant. He showed no affection, and he was quick with a death stare or a belt. Even though he was in the house, he wasn't involved in my life. But he taught me so much. I learned through watching and imitating, rather than him teaching me directly. When he did watch me, there was more criticism than encouragement. That's all I knew.

My dad was an athlete in high school, and he even had offers to play college football. So when I played sports in school — basketball and track and field — I would look in the stands and wonder why he was never there. I would see mom in the stands (she was my ride) until I got my license.

My dad played the guitar in a band when I was young. I thought that was pretty cool. At Christmas, he would even pull out his guitar and play for a while. When I was in my twenties, a comedy club opened in the city, and I had the bug. I performed stand-up for a short time, and I was doing well (if I say so myself). I thought, since we were both in the entertainment business, he would at least come to see me perform. He was a fan of Pryor, Foxx, Pigmeat Markham, Moms Mabley, and others, so I asked, and he said, "No." He did not offer an explanation. He just said, "No."

Don't get it twisted. I knew in his way that my dad loved me. But like most Black men in that era, that's just the way it was.

So, my friend's greeting from his dad was a shock for me. I decided at that moment that when I have children, they will know that I love them. My friend and I never talked about what I saw. But whenever I saw him and his dad together, I watched and studied. They actually enjoyed their time together.

Again, as my children grew, so did I. I tried to stay true to my word that they would know I loved them and I was proud of them.

But I still had to bring a little of my dad (the stare was effective), so they understood that I was also there to discipline when needed.

Please understand that I was not perfect. I had a daughter when I was young. And I wasn't ready to be a father. Regardless of my desire to be ready, I wasn't ready. So, of course, it wasn't always amicable between her mother and me.

When my daughter was about four or five, I moved to a different state for a job. I wish I'd had more time with her. I missed her extracurriculars. This is my biggest regret. But, I tried to make sure that if I could not be in her life physically, my mother and father were.

Although I wasn't there daily, she has grown into a strong, independent, beautiful Black woman, and that is all because of her mother. My daughter moved to my state and lives a few miles away from me. We're in contact at least once a week, and our relationship is strong.

My wife and I have twin sons. (Yeah, I know.) Man, finding out we were having twins…whew! My wife and I were pregnant and lost the baby. But we were pregnant again almost immediately. (Yeah, I'm grinnin'.) The doctors wanted to get an ultrasound to make sure everything was OK. While waiting for the doctor to set up, I noticed a poster on the wall of the different stages of development in each month of pregnancy. In the lower right-hand corner was a lone picture of twins. The doctor had started the ultrasound. I said to the doctor,

"You don't see twins in there, do ya… LOL!" The doc said, "Just sit down. Let's get started." (Uh oh)

When the two heartbeats came on the screen, I asked the doc if they had a video of the screen in another room. My mind was all over the place. Two of everything — cribs, car seats, diapers — you get where I'm going…

From the start, my relationship with my sons was different for a lot of reasons. Of course, beginning with the obvious, they're boys. By the time they were born, ten years had passed since my daughter was born. I was more prepared mentally for what was happening. Being present and involved with them day-to-day was the actual difference.

Everything I wanted from my dad was put to task every day. As much as I tried to give the love I have been telling you about, it was tough when they wouldn't sleep at night! It was truly a test of fatherhood. But God showed me I was ready. (He also had to show me a few times after that.)

When the twins got older, I changed jobs. I was a manager and management trainer for a national jewelry chain. My drive to the office was over an hour from home. I was also traveling for new store setups and training. There were nights I was so tired that I didn't even remember driving home. Even worse, I wasn't getting to spend any time with the twins. I would take them to daycare in the morning and try to get some sleep before going to work. When I got home at night, they were sleeping. But not for long, as I mentioned earlier.

After a couple of years, I changed jobs so I could see my family. I could then spend time with the boys in the mornings before daycare, and I was home at night to hang out with them. But all wasn't rosy. I had a weird schedule that caused me to work more weekends. And because of "seniority," the spring breaks and prime vacation times were always taken by people that had grown-ass kids!!! (Sorry. Still a little bitter.) I couldn't take vacations when it was time. That meant my wife would always take the boys on the trips alone. As a man and a father, I didn't like that. Not because I wasn't on the beach chillin'. It wasn't safe, and it really bothered me. But they survived, and my sons were introduced to my work ethic. They knew even though I wasn't on the beach, I was making it possible for them.

Today, they are in their twenties with jobs of their own. I see them every day getting up (yeah, they're still in my damn house), getting ready for work, arriving on time, and taking pride in what they do. I have tried to instill these traits in all three of my children. So far, so good.

It was important as the twins grew older to keep them involved. It was also important that they saw me when they looked in the stands. When they were in the band, I was there for the recitals (that was tough) or in the bleachers when they made free throws or extra-base hits. We eventually chose baseball (cause the band just wasn't workin').

I had an opportunity to be their coach, and it was a great time to bond. It also allowed us to improve our communication. We laughed (something my dad and I rarely did). We started watching baseball games and college basketball (our favorite) together. Even more conversation flowed, which led to a stronger comfort level within our relationships. It became easy for them to come to me for just about anything. (I later realized there were some things I didn't want or need to know.)

As the boys progressed at the game, they became pretty good. They started playing travel and high school ball and were getting attention from several colleges. It became clear this could get them an education. And it did.

Signing day was big for them and me. I was full of emotions, remembering all the days we had spent practicing in the yard, the trips we had taken all over the country to play ball, and all the money we had spent (I could've had a new truck.) All of this while they still maintained top grades in accelerated classes in school. And there we were, ready for the next phase.

And still learning.

Yep! Both attended an HBCU college on baseball scholarships. Now don't get it twisted, my sons were good. But as they sat at the table signing their letters of intent, I was not having visions of them playing in the Majors. (Well, maybe one.)

Knowing the pitfalls for college freshmen, their minds needed to stay focused on baseball. The focus was on getting up in the mornings to train, camaraderie, and maintaining their grades to play. They wouldn't have much time for "college trouble." And it worked…

Until it didn't.

They had some "college trouble." It was the call you never want as a parent. I explained that they needed to be careful of the people they allowed in their life, but they had to learn on their own. They were hemmed up because they were with a teammate who was knocking on the wrong apartment door looking for another teammate. It was the apartment of an elderly lady. Evidently, the teammate had words with the lady, and it led to the "popo" being called. They weren't taken to jail, but one of them was cuffed for some time.

Once we straightened out their situation and decided our next moves, my wife and I had a conference call with our sons and an administrator. The guidelines were laid out, and after listening to what had gone on and what the next steps were, the conversation ended, and I told my sons, "Hey guys, I love you." Their response was, "Love you too, Dad." And then there was silence. When the silence broke, the administrator sitting with my sons said, "Sir, I have never heard a man speak to his sons like that before. You never hear a man say I love you to his son." At that moment, the thought and feelings I had years before came back to me. The reflex to tell my sons I love them shocked someone else the way I was shocked decades ago by my friend and the greeting his father gave him.

When we went to the school to support our sons, talk to the administration, and receive their decision, we were the only parents in attendance. Before leaving, I hugged my sons and told them, "I love you." The administrator again spoke about the way we supported our sons. But for me, it was no question. Remember… anytime, anyplace.

I believe if I had any serious issues, my dad would have been there for me. But I didn't want to push it. I knew whatever trouble I was in would pale compared to what I would have dealt with at home with my dad.

I guess the short of it is that I never wanted my children to live in fear of me (as I did with my dad). I didn't want to receive or give love through fear. I wanted my sons to know I loved them, even when mistakes were made. No one is perfect, and I don't expect perfection from my sons.

Again learning.

When my children graduated from college, I found I needed to have different conversations with all of them. The conversation changed from, "No, don't do that," to, "If you do this, what things could happen?" I was now letting them discover through conversation and thought, not an ultimatum. But there will always be times when ultimatums are the only way, even for adults.

As your children grow older, continue influencing and encouraging them, as well as their friends and other youth you encounter. Encourage them to know their potential, talents, and strengths; to set high expectations for themselves. A dream cannot be seen, but the work that is needed to make a dream come true can be seen. Tell them to find their passion and let it drive them. Finally, teach them to fight for what they love and believe in. That is a conversation I wish I could have had with my father.

Fatherhood has its unique set of challenges. But as a Black man, they become even more unique. Especially when dealing with law enforcement. I know it's an old, tired conversation. But it is a conversation every Black man I know has had with his children, especially his sons. Sadly, it's a necessity.

My sons saw me go through it. Before you jump to conclusions, no, I don't have a record or warrants and no ties to criminal activity. We were on our way back to college with the twins. We were driving a new SUV and pulling a trailer. I noticed a trooper sitting on the side of the road. He jumped behind us and pulled us over for speeding! We were pulled over on a four-lane highway with a grass median for doing 45 mph in a 35-mph zone. (Let that sink in for a minute.) The trooper asked for my credentials, and he ran my license. I watched him look in and around the vehicle as he walked away. Everyone in the vehicle was quiet and maybe a little afraid. When he came back to the car, I was informed nothing came back, and he would let us go with a warning.

We talked about the incident later, and I made sure our sons understood they were just shown how to act and what to say to prevent the situation from escalating. A few years later, they saw what can happen on full display with George Floyd and Brianna Taylor. No, Mr. Floyd and Ms. Taylor were not pulled over by the police, but I wanted the twins to understand with any escalation, the outcome of any situation with law enforcement could have been the same. Along with the gift of fatherhood comes the dread of worry and the question, "Have I done enough to prepare them for this life?"

It's important as a father to understand that you cannot do it alone. There will be someone in your circle that you can talk to about what you're going through or dealing with. They may have had a similar experience.

I remember when I found out that we were having twins. I was at my friend's house, sitting in his garage (the same friend years ago I went on a day trip with that changed my life). We liked to play table tennis (something we picked up in college). He had a son at the time that was a toddler, and I told him then that I was worried about fatherhood. I was worried because I wanted to be a better father to my sons than my father was to me. Again, my father was a great provider. That wasn't the issue. I wanted to make sure my sons knew I was there and that I loved them. I didn't have that relationship with my daughter at the time, so it was imperative that I had it with them. My friend was on the road I was about to get on. He assured me it would be fine, not easy, but fine, and they will know.

It's tough to find that person. We, as men, don't want to seem soft, like we can't handle a situation. But it's important to find that person. It could be a 40-year or 4-month friendship. You will find them.

My mother always told me, "Talk to your father. You're going to miss him when he's gone." She was right. As I reflect on my time with my father, I'm thankful for all I learned from him. I learned to provide for my family, be a good and quick judge of people, work with my hands, etc. I hope that someday my children will look back and feel they learned from me. I pray they understand the importance of family. My twins understand that being a man, and a father, has great responsibility, and my way was a blueprint, not the building. They can build it any way they see fit. Just make sure it stands.

There are at least ten definitions in the dictionary for what a father is. But the only one who can determine what a father should be — is you.

When you are ready, not just financially, but as a spiritual leader, confidant, teacher, and disciplinarian, you will help determine the trajectory the youth in your life take.

Remember, as your children grow, so do you.

Now, as I look back, I pray that my actions have influenced the people I have encountered positively. I pray the moment at school with my sons opened the eyes of that administrator, just as mine were opened years before on that day trip, and I pray they develop love in their relationships.

I've been told that whatever you go through in life is not for you but for you to help someone else. I pray that has happened.

Iron sharpens iron.

Daniel Vasquenza

Dan Vasquenza is a native New Englander and honors graduate of Southern New Hampshire University, where he majored in Business Administration with a minor in Marketing. Dan owns and operates his business, VazMan, a sales and marketing firm based in Georgia. Dan's professional background includes award-winning sales activity in marketing big brands with professional sports teams and athletes through trademarks, sponsorship, advertising, and media assets. His work has represented all four major professional sports leagues (NBA, NFL, MLB, and NHL) and some notable athletes.

Before starting VazMan, Dan served five seasons leading sponsorship and premium hospitality sales activity for the NBA's Atlanta Hawks. While with the Hawks, Dan approached one of their owners and a mega entrepreneur for mentoring. Their perspective on life and fatherhood has resonated with Dan's approach as a single dad to his special needs son, Jack.

Dan's ongoing non-profit work with KultureCity, alongside Chairman-NBA Hall of Famer-Top 75 Player of all time, Dominique Wilkins, has further influenced his philosophy on fatherhood and humanity. This global organization aligns with Dan's values in giving back to communities while providing a significant platform to help create a world of acceptance and inclusion for individuals with sensory needs. Serving others is especially near and dear to Dan and Jack.

Dan's greatest joy is his role as a father. Dan's other passions include spending time with his family and friends, traveling, running, exploring nature, live music, working out, and the family dog, Otter.

CHAPTER 5

The Shared Bond of Father, Son, and Community

Daniel Vasquenza

I t was late morning on July 31, 2004. Unexpectedly, I found myself with a slight panic seated in a very bright room surrounded by a team of professionals in Boston, Ma. My life was about to change forever. This experience would be much bigger than my beloved Red Sox trading away the face of the franchise, Nomar Garciaparra, on this very same date. Seriously, that was big, ultimately ending the Boston Red Sox's 86-year world series drought with multiple championships to follow. Yes, this was huge, giving me the greatest job title of all time, welcoming my son Jack Clayton Vasquenza into the world. It was  just like that; I have a child and instantly became a dad, a member of the ultimate club of amazing men that symbolize leadership in communities and families.

As parents, our kids need our strength, modeling, and, more importantly, our presence. I want to be sure my presence and quality time with Jack is substantial. I learned this at a young age, and it came with a painful lesson that would ultimately fuel me as a dad. I was ten years old when my mom and dad split up. I thought my dad was coming home, and he didn't. My parents later divorced, and my mom found herself raising three kids while juggling two full-time jobs. As I reflect on my mom's sacrifices, she will forever be my hero and No. 1 Wonder Woman. It was truly my mom's actions during those tough times that modeled lessons for me about the value of responsibility, accountability, drive, and work ethic. Those lessons ultimately became my foundational guide during my teenage years into adulthood.

My dad stayed in contact with me during those years, but it was limited. He lived in Florida and later moved to California, where his job had him moving and living for short stints around the southeast. He missed a lot of my growing pains and gains that go along with being a teenager. Yes, and that included my tough teenage behavior with my mom. He also missed the fun and celebrations of me playing sports, growing up, and just maturing. Those experiences guided me into adulthood and motivated me as a dad - that is, to be present.

Jack's Journey

As a toddler, there were signs of Jack's delayed development. One very noticeable milestone was he didn't walk until he was 22 months. Although with the overachiever in Jack, it was more like a run than a walk. During Jack's preschool years, delays became more noticeable in his motor skills, speech, and overall response time. At age five, Jack received a free evaluation through the county school system and was diagnosed with autism. We'd later pay for a professional weeklong evaluation which would diagnose Jack with several learning disabilities (LPD, LD, AD, ADHD, etc.). We essentially saw a lot of the alphabet in his evaluation but nothing about autism. Within minutes of meeting Jack, the Psychologist ruled out any diagnosis of autism. She defined the core of autism as less engagement and concluded by saying, "Jack is very engaging, charming, and very funny with a good sense of humor." It was great to get some answers, but I wasn't satisfied. The process of that evaluation was external. I was uneasy, not knowing what was going on internally.

On November 30, 2013, I had a pair of tickets to "Clean, Good Old-Fashioned Hate." This translates into the hottest college football tickets of the season if you live in the South. Jack was super excited because he was going to see his Yellow Jackets play at Bobby Dodd Stadium. It was a beautiful autumn day. The Georgia Tech Yellow Jackets were hosting their rivals, the University of Georgia Bulldogs. Jack had been to several Tech football games since we moved from Boston to Georgia in 2006. During that time, I worked for the Georgia Tech flagship radio station, 790 The Zone. As a result, Jack became a well-seasoned and experienced fan. For this particular game, our seats were in a different location, but of course, I thought nothing of it until later.

Jack and I arrived with enough time to get into our seats before kick-off. As we moved through the crowd toward our seats, I noticed Jack started moving slower. I then reminded Jack what I said to him earlier in our car ride, "You're going to love these seats Daddy's friend got for us." As we continued, I wondered about his hesitation and then said, "Jack, come on buddy, let's get to our seats before the game starts to hear the national anthem." I learned from attending previous sporting events how much Jack loves the national anthem. I also learned something else that day that would change our lives forever.

Despite Jack moving slower than usual, he assured me he didn't need the bathroom or anything to eat. So, we grabbed each other's hands, walked through the stadium tunnel, and down the aisle to our seats. I could feel his hand getting clammy and tighter as we ascended all the way to row 16. "Ok Jack, here's our row, shuffle past the people, say excuse me, our seats are in the middle, look for numbers 22 and 23," I said to him. Jack then gave me this bewildered look. "Oh boy," I thought, I know this look. It was terror. I didn't understand why. Prime seats, 16-rows up from the field, his favorite team, and we're on the sunny side. What a perfect day. Then he unleashed his terror as soon as we got to our seats. This became a full-on meltdown in the middle of the crowd, including some of my friends. Suddenly, nothing else mattered.

It was Jack's siren saying, *"Get me out of here."* Careful not to draw more attention, we quickly and discreetly climbed up the steps into the concourse. As we moved off to the side, Jack tried to decompress while we huddled in a corner away from the crowd. At that moment, I had to make the right but hard decision to leave Bobby Dodd Stadium immediately. Jack wanted so much to see the game. We'd later learn his senses went on overload that day, and it was a life-changing experience and the impetus to pursuing a deeper diagnosis.

Flash ahead to July 8, 2015 - I'm seated in the Atlanta Emory Health Clinic waiting room, and my nerves are simmering as I anxiously anticipate the diagnosis from Jack's blood work. I'll never forget the words the doctor spoke to his mom and me upon entering the room. "Well, you should know that you have certainly hit the *jackpot* with Jack." No pun, it left me gazing back at her waiting to hear the word, *"BUT,"* which she never said. As I continued listening to the doctor, I drifted into an out-of-body experience when she proclaimed Jack's diagnosis, *"Chromosome 18p deletion."*

Chromosome 18p deletion is a rare chromosome abnormality in which there is a deletion of all or part of the short arm (p) chromosome 18 (www.chromosome18.org).

Essentially, Jack is missing pieces of the 67 genes that make chromosome 18, which supports development and function. Jack's diagnosis was a celebration of defining the unknown, just as we may associate a celebration, including gifts. Jack is truly a gift; he brings them to me and the people he meets every day. Although initially, I wasn't feeling a "Ya-hoo" moment. Instead, I was overwhelmed, filled with fear, uneducated, and had an overall feeling of helplessness. Aren't we dads supposed to protect our young? I rode an unwanted rollercoaster of emotions that we typically go through when experiencing something dramatically stressful. It may not have been like losing a loved one, but it was within proximity. I did a good job hiding my emotions from people for roughly a year. Then I met my tribe by joining the Chromosome 18 Registry & Research Society.

On July 10, 2016, I attended their annual conference in San Antonio, TX. I went alone to focus on the conference materials and meet others in our new community. I arrived for check-in at the San Antonio Marriott Rivercenter Hotel. Two things instantly gave me perspective. As I scanned the lobby floor, it was swarming with kids and parents smiling from ear to ear. Suddenly, the word *"jackpot"* rang loud in my ear just as the Emory doctor had proclaimed Jack's diagnosis. Yep, her explanation became crystal clear. Gratitude hugged me like a comforting blanket. I felt tears running down my cheeks, realizing we're much more fortunate than some other families.

While there are still times I feel alone, I must continue to remind myself that I have a community that can help me tackle most challenges in parenting Jack as a single dad. Frankly, I learned most of those challenges aren't as difficult as those others face.

Dads – Parents, We All Develop Our Style

I believe fatherhood is one of the most rewarding, difficult, and important responsibilities you will ever experience that requires consistent sacrifice and selfless output. Although parenting styles may be "different strokes for different folks," we all have one thing in common: two people decided to bring someone into this world. Now, it's on us dads to ***love, guide, inspire, serve, celebrate, and nurture* them into adulthood.** Certainly, there may be other useful action words to best describe the role of dads, but for now, I've chosen these to align with my experiences.

We feel <u>LOVE</u> inside for our children, and it's vital that we give it all to them.

I felt the love instantly when the nurse handed Jack to me for the first time. I vividly remember him swaddled in his blanket, propped on my lap as we gazed into each other's eyes. The world literally stopped at that very moment. At least it felt that way to me. My heart swelled up with love the size of a hot-air balloon and felt like nothing I'd ever experienced before. Of course, a feeling of love has many types of emotions and expressions uniquely felt through each meaningful interaction. However, we all agree the love for a child is truly selfless and pure. I would highly recommend Dr. Gary Chapman's book, *"The Five Love Languages."* Although it's best known for its practical use for couples, it's a resourceful application for communication in any relationship. You just may find it helpful to understand what language styles resonate for you and your child to better align in your communication. It was fascinating to learn how one of these languages guides Jack. "Quality Time" is Jack's dominant language and aligns consistently with our interactions. I hope you enjoy discovering your own and your child's love language.

While we're loving and being present as dads, we must <u>GUIDE</u> our children to thrive into adulthood.

Typically, parents focus on guiding behavior through encouragement and discouragement. But motivation certainly plays a role in determining how you guide, just as the old saying goes, "carrot or the stick." When you consistently set clear, reasonable limits with love and support, you are guiding or teaching managed behavior. You must also be aware of what you say, how you say it, and what you do to properly guide the behavior you're seeking. Tone, delivery, and modeling are three key takeaways from becoming a "guided champion." I've not yet become the guided champion I'd like to be for Jack. Although, I've found taking deep breaths and counting helps tremendously. I really mean being intentional about encouraging the behavior I want and discouraging the unwanted outputs from Jack. Certainly, that may sound simple, but not so fast. It's tough and sometimes we must give tough love while recognizing their motivation. Here is where Jack and I differ in the "carrot and stick." Jack is a "carrot" all the time, while I say bring on the stick (please note the analogy). Be sure their motivation aligns with your guidance. Of course, these strategies are most effective if you're present with your kids.

The strong building block is when motivation comes from inspiration.

Be the one to <u>INSPIRE</u> your children

> *"When we reach for the heart in a way that the person changes from the inside out, that will make it sustainable and lead to long-term vibrancy (*)."*

I also believe we must first be inspired to inspire others. The absence of my dad was about him not being a physical presence in the home where our family grew up in Connecticut. More to come in this chapter about a father figure in the home. I did get to see my dad occasionally, and strangely this became my inspiration. Remember, I had thought he was coming home. When I realized he wasn't, I had to channel that emotion of hurt and disappointment. This shift became a mindset toward looking forward to the moments I would have with my dad—an old school phone call, his letter in the mailbox (yup, no internet back then), or us getting together. These interactions became my inspiration to share "good things" happening in my life. This may not be a traditional way of a father's motivation for his child, but it was mine, and it later became my fuel. A child just really wants to make his dad proud, and that was certainly my inspiration.

As Jack's dad, he reminds me to flip that script of inspiration by listening to and understanding the things that are important to him. Sports (especially baseball), Atlanta Braves, Wiffleball, weather, Minecraft, learning new things, family, and his friends are just a few things Jack is passionate about. All of Jack's passions motivate me to create experiences for him that we've done and continue to do together. Although looking back, I'm still trying to figure out who's having more fun. For now, we'll continue this journey until he tells me otherwise. This includes Jack's dream to visit every Major League Baseball Park or stadium. As a dad, it's invaluable to give our kids something to look forward to doing together. As well, having them experience something you're passionate about might truly inspire them.

When motivation and inspiration intersect into <u>SERVICE</u> for others, that's when the real magic happens.

I witnessed the value of service to others growing up. Looking back, I would say I was lucky to have the best of both worlds in my life. It was Stan (a.k.a. Buddy) who instilled a great lesson. Actions speak "in love" louder than words. I added a couple of words to that very popular phrase, and I like it. I hope you do too.

It became official on May 26, 1991, when Stan Johnson and my mom, Valerie, got married. Prior to this date, there were several examples of fatherhood and a man's commitment to service for those he loves. As for the earlier reference to Dr. Chapman's book, *"The Five Love Languages,"* Stan is hands down the "Acts of Service" MAN! He'd make a good poster boy for that entire chapter. It was his acts of service that showed up every day in every way that gave me a strong sense of security. Fix it, change it, come get it, and always be there is a great way to summarize Buddy's involvement. Trust me, he brought a broader definition of the things to fix or get involved in. He attended a good amount of my sporting events straight through high school football and basketball.

One event that recently happened really sticks with me. I mentioned earlier that I joined the Chromosome 18 Registry & Research Society. This organization inspired me to raise awareness and funds. I wanted to accomplish something physically hard with a #18 theme. It was during Covid that I set a challenge to go 80 miles on foot in less than 18 hours. I called it the 18/80 run challenge and set out to accomplish this triumph in a confined area. I chose a new commuter parking lot that was recently built near my house and was part of my training route. I later realized going 80 miles might be a daunting task for someone that hadn't even run a full marathon.

On April 18, 2021, Buddy, the MAN, was there from the 5:30 a.m. start to the 9:36 p.m. finish. He helped set up tents, complete some errands, and literally sat to watch me lap around a parking lot 195 times. As always, he didn't need to say anything. He was there in his caring and reliable way.

Let me tell you, humanity is good. People stepped up to support us. I'm forever grateful to those who assisted in helping raise over $24,000. Jack and I did videos on social media promoting the run and his unique qualities to celebrate our tribe and anyone classified as having a "disability."

Buddy's presence and service over many years is truly a gift that I'm so grateful he chooses to do for me, our family, and the people he loves. His acts of service are a foundational trait exemplified in my being a dad to Jack that has also carried over into my non-profit work.

KultureCity (www.kulturecity.org) is a non-profit organization I'm personally connected to, which inspires me to further serve individuals like Jack. KultureCity is the leading non-profit for acceptance and inclusion in serving individuals with sensory needs. Sensory Needs are the most common traits for individuals with autism, PTSD, mental health, dementia, rare chromosome abnormalities, etc. I was introduced to KultureCity while working for the Atlanta Hawks and State Farm Arena. After completing KultureCity's certification employee training program, I became interested in their mission. Later, I had done some work for them and was asked to join their board of directors alongside NBA Hall of Famer, Top 75 Players of All-time, and Chairman of the Board, Dominique Wilkins.

Our primary focus at KultureCity is to make public places safe spaces for individuals with sensory needs to attend and thrive. However, our certification training program has grown to train local-state governments and public municipalities such as first responders - police, fire, EMTs, and 9-1-1 operators. As our certification grows into other sectors, KultureCity is making huge strides toward broadening its impact. After serving KultureCity's Board for over two years, I recently stepped down to do more fundraising for them.

Dads serve in many ways. Consider some of the things you're doing. How are you serving? What could you amplify to affect others? If this is not you, where might you get started today and build momentum?

"CELEBRATE good times! Come on!"

Just as the song goes, "Celebrate" by Kool & the Gang is a good reminder to actively acknowledge both the everyday *and* extraordinary accomplishments of our kids. My definition of any future "celebrating," at least as a dad, changed at the Atlanta Emory Health Clinic. But with Jack's diagnosis, there are many milestones to be recognized and celebrated along the way. My emphasis with Jack is on celebrating the sweat equity he puts into every challenge or milestone rather than focusing on results. He understands things, it just might take a little longer than the average person his age to finish or get things right.

I often worry if the world will accept and include Jack as he gets older. I'm super concerned for his future and others like him that may potentially be discriminated against for just being different. There have been hardships, sacrifices, and challenges for me as a single dad. However, celebrating differences teaches love, acceptance, and inclusion. I'm hopeful others will join this celebration of differences by creating a greater understanding in communities. By this, we enable Jack and others like him to strive toward living an independent life, just like everyone else. No doubt, the world will become a better place when we stop to see things through their eyes.

Identify that balance of **NURTURING** for growth and ultimate connection

The *"Super Soul Sunday"* podcast with Oprah Winfrey became my tune-in some mornings while commuting to Atlanta for work. I recall an episode with Dr. Shefali Tsabary about this very topic of celebrating our children. She explains how parents have been conditioned to only celebrate their children accomplishing big things while missing the important little victories. She suggests those moment-to-moment instances when our children demonstrate habits and behaviors, we're aiming to reinforce are perfect occasions to make connections.

Connection is about relationships, and the most important relationships require nurturing. Every human has common basic needs and desires. We want to be seen, understood, and celebrated for who we are, even more than our successes. Our children need to know they matter, and we can meet them there through nurturing. Don't misunderstand nurturing for baby stuff. Nurturing continues through our entire adult life and into the relationships we value most — our children. Don't get me wrong, at times I may have done too much "baby stuff" nurturing Jack. It's a struggle, at least for me, knowing he is going through so much trying to fit into the world. So, I compensate by helping him with stuff that I should allow him to do on his own.

Growth happens by doing uncomfortable things. I need to get better at letting Jack experience some struggles in various tasks that make him uncomfortable. I'm working on it. What are some things you're nurturing to grow your relationship and connection with your kids? Also, like me, what are some nurturing things, you need to let go of for them to grow?

How did we do as Dads?

There's no road map for parenting, especially for a child with special needs. It's truly blazing your path through trial and error. I've had days where I've nailed it as a parent and other days sitting alone in a dark closet crying, trying to figure it out. I believe we don't know how we did as parents until our children become adults themselves. Somewhere between the ages of 26 and 28 is where adulthood seems to take shape. Regardless of the timeline, I'm a believer that with a growth mindset, people (yes, even adult children) can change at any point in time. But that's a subject for another book.

For now, we're grateful you chose our book to become a better parent. Congratulations on being a much better parent because you are. YOU CARE! You care for your child, and you care to get better as a parent. For that, I celebrate you! Thank you for reading my chapter. I look forward to hearing from you and learning more about your journey as a mom, a dad, or both.

My son Jack has come a long way since his meltdowns. He is currently a rising senior at Kennesaw Mountain High School. He aspires to get his college degree and become a meteorologist and dog trainer. It's hard to predict his future, but I'm hopeful he'll forever carry his joy for life toward living independently one day. That's all I care and think about while trying to be the best dad for Jack. I don't always get it right, but Jack, you are right for this world and deserve the best. I love you, Jack Clayton Vasquenza, and I LOVE being your dad.

Lastly, I'd like to dedicate this final paragraph to the memory of my dad, Michael Anthony Vasquenza. Dad, I know you did your best. I hope I made you proud and know I'm trying every day while I continue to pray to you for your continued inspiration.

*Source: Lead X By Robb Holman (11:06:17)

**Source: Chromosome 18 registry and research society publicized website

Juan Alarcon

Juan Alarcon was born in Colombia in 1971 and immigrated to the US with his family during childhood. His loving parents and five siblings were heavily influential in his life as he grew up, and the bond between him and his family has only grown stronger through the years. Juan and his wife, Natalia, have a twenty-one-year-old and an eighteen-year-old son. They have raised them to be God-fearing men who appreciate the little things in life and understand the value of hard work and sacrifice.

Juan graduated from Georgia State University and has been with the same company for over 27 years. He has been nationally recognized for many years for his work in the dental-technology industry. He continues to break company sales records solely due to his grit and lovable personality.

Juan is a man that gets things done without taking life too seriously. The most important decision he makes daily is to be in a good mood, and he stands as a pillar of love, joy, and loyalty for many. Juan attributes his career success to "not prioritizing his career success." Instead, his devotion to God and dedication to his family are of utmost importance, and this orientation of values guides him through life. Juan is proud of his time as a father, and he is grateful to have had the privilege of this role. He continues to impact many people's lives, work hard towards his responsibilities, and (most importantly) make sure he has fun while doing it.

CHAPTER 6

Principle & Love: A Beautiful Balancing Act

Juan Alarcon

The scene is from an 80s cult classic movie: the big, loud family packs into the station wagon with wood panels on the side. The hot southern sun glistens on dad's aviators, and pregnant mom tames the five kids in the back with quick-witted commands in Spanish. I sat in the last row facing the back of the car, watching the road shrink into the horizon as we headed towards our new home in the United States. Within seconds, my daydream was interrupted by my big sister's bra hurtling through the air on the highway, then my socks and Dad's Speedos that should have never seen the light of day. In a gust of wind, the rest of my family's wardrobe  had escaped the roof-rack luggage container and littered the interstate during rush hour.

For the next 35 minutes, we watched our dad play dodge-the-car from the side of the highway as he picked up our clothes from the ground. It was a hell of a sight, especially for an eight-year-old. At that age, I couldn't grasp the gravity of that day—the sacrifices my father unquestionably offered and the course that my life was set on from that day forward. As I reminisce on this four decades later, I'm consumed by gratitude, humility, and pride. I look back and see a father—my father—venturing into the abyss of opportunity and confronting risk with faith that his kids will live better lives than his.

The new life that my dad gifted me began at Soap Creek elementary school in 1979. Being one of the first Hispanic kids to walk the halls defaulted me as prey for the class bully. I was raised in a tumultuous household where self-assured toughness was required, so the dull teasing did little damage. However, once the harassment escalated, I sought guidance at home. Dad was on business trips more often than not, so mom offered much-needed advice. "My love," she gently said in Spanish, "if he keeps bothering you, just punch him in the nose." Like the good son I was, I obeyed my mother and clocked the kid in the face. My decision landed me in detention—a small price to pay for the grand victory I had secured and the lesson I had learned about independence.

The demand for my self-sufficiency persisted throughout my childhood. My dad spent most of his time away from home, working to provide for our family. I was the man of the house and had no choice but to take on that responsibility. My mother was busy raising six kids, keeping God ever-present in our lives, and preserving the harmony in our family. I was not neglected, and not once did I feel that way. Being a victim was a luxury I could not afford and a mindset my family would not tolerate. Love flooded every square inch of my home, and my parents set an example to be followed.

My father's example was hard work, sacrifice, resilience, grit, respect, dependability, and an unwavering dedication to God. The lessons he taught me molded me into the young man I became and will stay with me for the rest of my life. He believed in principles—simple, fundamental rules that served as a foundation. "Greet adults properly. Look at them in their eyes, and keep a firm handshake," was a practice that dad chiseled into my behavior. Those lessons are the immortalized form of my dad's spirit that has been passed through me to my kids and will continue down the generations through the vessel of fatherhood. My father's example taught me what to do, but because of his humanity and inevitable flaws, some of his decisions also taught me what not to do. My dad's hard work paid off in abundance and funded the lifestyle my family and I were privileged with. However, to his detriment, my father adopted a shortsighted financial mindset that would burden him for the rest of his life. As long as money poured in, twice as much would drain out. Retirement, savings, and rainy-day funds were a concern for tomorrow, and the depth of the hole he dug was finally too deep to be escaped alone. The demand for my self-sufficiency matured into a responsibility greater than myself. It was 1994, and I was a Georgia State University student when I realized it was time for tough love. I addressed the situation, realized the work that needed to be done, and helped my dad preserve his business and our family's financial stability. I now understand that I was given the childhood, the parents, and the lessons I learned for a purpose. My father did his duty as a father, and I did mine as a son so that one day I would be a formidable pillar for others to rely on—a testament to what fatherhood means to me. To prepare my boys for the world, for the unbearable suffering and surreal beauty life offers, is what I am here to do.

I love my dad. He did his best. Now my job is to be better than his best and for my kids to be better than that. It's a matter of recognizing that I am not just a seed becoming a tree but a small part of a massive, ever-evolving forest. My purpose as a father is not limited to the time I'm on the earth—it transcends the parameters we bind ourselves to. I am a part of an incomprehensibly beautiful cycle of love, wisdom, and God Himself flowing through generations. However, thinking about the existential meaning of being a dad is not how I spend most of my time parenting. My time is spent waking up before my kids to make their favorite breakfast, quesadillas. Being a father is working my ass off to give my boys the peace of financial stability and *knowing* when to set aside work to watch their high school tennis match. "Everything in moderation, buddy" is an axiom my boys have heard from me more than once, and though this is something we fail to practice when my wife bakes cookies, it's wisdom that has guided me in this journey. Like any purposeful endeavor, success is a symphony that must be mindfully orchestrated and persistently tended to. If one part of the grand band slacks off, the music begins to die. Being a good father is inherently intertwined with being a good husband, a good son, a good worker, and a good man of God. No success at the office or anywhere else can compensate for failure at home.

The man I am today cannot be solely attributed to my father's teachings or my own wits. My mom led the day-to-day parenting during my childhood, and her determination to raise good children was immovable. Her parenting was intentional and goal-oriented. The question was, "what are the most important ways my sons can serve others?" Her answer followed: "become the best husbands and fathers they can be." This mission was rooted in her understanding of the importance of family. The synergy of our Colombian culture and Catholic faith established that a sturdy family was the bedrock of a fruitful life; thus, finding a way to contribute to this structure was vital. As a child, my mother did not simply wave her finger and tell me to prepare to be a dad. Her parenting style embodied faith, discipline, and unconditional love; her authority was non-negotiable, while her fairness was just. She encouraged us to be kids that climbed trees and scraped knees because she knew that the sanctity of childhood needed to be nurtured. In other words, we were allowed to be kids—as long as we followed the rules.

Discipline and respect were embedded in the structure of our home because raising six kids without those two principles would be utter chaos. The discipline was instilled in us through responsibilities ranging from yard work and cleaning the pool to excelling in school and translating English for my mom at the DMV. At a young age, I was a part of a family—a system, a structure—that depended on me as I did on it, and any failure to do my duties would result in swift consequences. The demand for respect came from our Colombian culture. Any adult entering our home was to be greeted and acknowledged properly (regardless of age), and shyness was not tolerated. Our manners were taught at home because my mother knew she was responsible for preparing us for society. These lessons taught me how to carry myself confidently and navigate social situations smoothly; I ask myself how drastically different I would be if I had not had my mother.

Mom's tough love was complemented by her tender generosity. Her eagerness to give, and give, and give was the example she set for us. There was no stranger unworthy of her love, and there was no deed too big to do. Relatives, friends, friends of friends, and priests that immigrated to the United States were invited to stay in our home until they got on their feet. Mom ventured into war-torn regions of Colombia to create safe houses for kids to intercept the flow of children into a life of crime. Through her, I realized that the value of money, material wealth, and privilege was savored when given to others—not when it was coveted or hoarded. Mom was a beacon for us and for many, and that begs the question: what was *her* beacon?

She answered this question before saying a word. Simply looking at my mom showed you the rock on which she stood and the light that guided all of her decisions. A small pendant of the Virgin Mary rested on her forehead, a cross hung around her neck, and a colorful combination of butterflies and flowers would be printed on her clothes. Catholic insignia covered the walls of our home, and prayer was a daily routine. She was our family's spiritual leader and used a religious framework to provide structure in our family and in the way she raised us. This gave us stability and gave me a guide to fatherhood.

As I grow older, face more challenges, and try more things, I realize the need for knowledge. I look back at my mom and dad to gather the elements of their parenting I would like to carry on. I seek what to do and not to do by observing my peers raising their children, and I also use my experience as a guide to fatherhood. However, after more than two decades of being a father, the Bible is the source of knowledge I resort to the most without fail. So, to any young father reading my words in search of guidance: read the Bible. When doubt and despair contaminate your mind, read the Bible. When you are challenged as a husband or a father, and the foundations of your life are shaken, read the Bible. This advice can be easily dismissed as a cliche regurgitated by grandmothers and religious leaders alike. However, I compel you to ask, "Why has this book survived for thousands of years, and why have billions of people believed in it?" The integrity of the Bible's knowledge is irrelevant to what you believe in. These words have outlived the world's most powerful empires, economic systems, social structures, and ideologies. What common ground have billions of people maintained for thousands of years other than religion? Regardless of your beliefs, I assure you that abiding by the guidance in the Bible (to any degree) *will* benefit you. Whether you decide only to employ the good old "love your neighbor as yourself" (Mark 12:31), or if you embrace the entire scripture, good will come. I make this spirited claim not only as a Christian but as a father, too.

An integral piece of wisdom in the Bible addresses the importance of discipline when raising a child. The words read: "He who spares the rod hates his son, but he who loves him is diligent to discipline him" (Proverbs 13:24). I raised my two sons with clear, simple rules that merited punishment when broken. The rules were not complicated nor abundant and were based on principle, reason, and the Bible. "Obey your mom and me, no matter what. Be respectful to adults. Be kind and grateful" were among the fundamental rules in our home. Enforcing these rules was a matter of encouraging good behavior and discouraging bad behavior effectively. For my boys (and for most kids), a ten-minute "time out" or a suspension of "screen time" was not enough to discourage them from misbehaving. When the situation called for it, my sons received a spanking from my wife or myself to enforce the rules and punish any behavior that should not be repeated. Spanking is an effective form of discipline when used properly and *not* abused. Parents should never spank their children out of anger and must take time to cool off before administering the punishment. It should be clear to the child why they are receiving the spanking and what they can do to avoid it next time. A spanking should *never* be fueled by impulse or frustration— it must be guided by tough love and an understanding of what is good for your child in the long run.

My boys, my wife, and I reaped the benefits of intentional discipline. As my sons grew older, they were free *because* they were disciplined. My wife and I entrusted them with more responsibility and liberty because we knew we had taken the time to instill a deep sense of right and wrong into them, thus giving us peace of mind. Parents who are afraid to discipline and instead prioritize their child's comfort, pleasure, and impulses ultimately do a disservice to the family as a whole. A child raised with blurry boundaries and unenforced principles will struggle to abide by the rules of the real world, and the parents will need to attend to every decision their child makes in fear that it might be the bad one. Disciplining is not easy, and it is not enjoyable. It is a challenge to put aside the tender love and awe my child inspires in me and replace it with tough love and sternness. However, love guided me the whole way.

A common mistake in parenting is trying to be your kid's friend. It is not our job to be our kid's pals—they will find some on their own. Attempting this kind of relationship with your child will create a conflict when it is time to be a parent who must do unfriendly things. Leveling yourself as a buddy to your child inherently contradicts your authority as their parent and blurs the boundaries of a healthy parent-child dynamic. However, a parent should not be a power-hungry tyrant, either. As a father, I worked to strike a balance between camaraderie and authority by fostering trust, dependability, and respect. Your child should not be afraid to tell you about their mistakes or doubt whether they can call you during a time of need. They must also understand that you are their parent who enforces rules for their well-being, and they need to acknowledge that through obedience. I was not my children's friend during their childhood, so I could be one of their best friends during adulthood. I raised boys to be men who I adore and admire and whose company I genuinely enjoy. As they enter adulthood, I can relieve myself of many of my fatherly duties and trust that I did my job as a dad well.

A series of fundamental principles have been constant during my time as a father, and my kids have grasped their gravity. One of the high priorities is, and always will be: "if you do something, do it well." When the dishes are done, clean them carefully, and put them away properly. When committing to a sport, put in the effort and be the best you can be. During school, engage in class and understand the value of getting good grades. I make sure to follow the advice I give, too. There is no purpose in putting in half the effort—it only degrades your work ethic and devalues your potential. Doing things well makes life easier, and halfway effort makes life harder. Jobs done halfway are precisely that: a job left with the other half undone. The load is inevitably placed on someone else or your future self, creating disorder that could have been avoided. While raising my kids, I made sure to show them what this axiom looked like when applied financially, too.

When my boys began to make money, whether from birthday gifts or mowing the neighbor's lawn, we made a habit of sitting down at the end of the week and allocating their earnings into three envelopes. The first envelope was designated for saving, the second for spending, and the third for donating. This simple practice fostered a foundation for financial organization and responsibility. That short-term sacrifice could provide long-term value was made clear, and the responsibility to give when you receive was made evident. There was no need for lengthy lectures or overbearing demands to teach financial wisdom; simple and persistent parenting gave my kids the resources they needed to learn and apply the newfound knowledge.

I do my best as a father. It is one of the most rewarding roles, and I'm proud of the two young men my wife and I raised. Despite the pat on my back, there are things I would have done differently. Responsibility and self-sufficiency are qualities I should have fostered more in my children as I raised them. This is not to say that they do not embody these two attributes, but I realize that there are things I could have done (or not done) as a father to instill those two qualities more effectively. In other words, I wish I would have done less for my kids— which is a thought that seems brash and counterintuitive at first glance.

Shouldn't parents do everything they possibly can for their kids? No, they shouldn't. Put simply, my job as a father is to love my children for who they are and to prepare them for the real world. I allude back to my motto, "everything in moderation," as I highlight the importance of tempering the paternal urge to provide for your kids. The ideal balance entails preparing and providing for your kids well enough so they can confront challenges in life. Over-providing for your kids will unmotivate them to push their boundaries and try new things since the easier option will always be made available by mom and dad. In application, this may be as simple as assigning chores at a young age, teaching them how to cook for themselves so they can make a proper meal independently, and showing them how to manage their finances. Instilling responsibility and self-sufficiency in your child is a matter of making the most of a learning opportunity and giving them the resources they need to venture into the unknown.

I was not prepared to be a father, and I know I would have never felt prepared enough to take on this daunting role. The idea of raising another human being that would completely depend on my wife and me was terrifying, humbling, exciting, and beautiful all at the same time. There was no amount of seminars, books, or pep talks that could convince me that I was ready to be a dad—and that is ok. I realized that preparedness was not the feeling to pursue when transitioning into fatherhood because preparedness is a feeling that is only about me. I drew my confidence as a father from elements in my life that bolstered me and, in turn, could guide me during this journey. My religion gave me a surefire framework that I could always refer to in times of doubt. My family offered unwavering support and dependability. My knowledge and principles were anchors that stopped me from drifting. However, the guiding light, the buoyancy, the devotion, and the most essential source of strength I had as I traversed fatherhood was my wife.

Looking for my life partner began with looking for the mother of my children. I sought a combination of qualities that my future kids would benefit from, and it just so happened that these qualities were everything I wanted in my wife. I needed dependability and loyalty, someone who knew the value of family and loved God, and a woman who thinks independently and acts intentionally. She counterbalances elements of who I am and ultimately makes me better because her strengths complement my inadequacies while her values parallel mine. My wife is everything I have ever needed and more. As we grew closer and transitioned into the beautiful marriage we have now, I had no doubt I would be the best father I could be *because* of her. You must realize that choosing your partner is choosing the parent of your unborn children; this realization will only clarify a sliver of the monumental impact your partner will have on your life and your family's life.

Parenting is the most difficult, demanding, and meaningful thing I have ever done. Having my wife, whom I trust to traverse parenthood with me, has been integral to my success as a father and has fortified our marriage. I acknowledge the challenge single parents face when raising their kids, and I admire their grit and dedication, despite their unimaginable challenges. I have been blessed with a beautiful marriage and a healthy wife, and I reap the benefits of this blessing every single day. Parenting alongside my wife has been a fruitful journey full of new lessons, and I have found a handful of these lessons to be vital.

The most important thing I can do for my kids is to be a good husband to my wife. A healthy marriage is a precondition to my ability as a father, and it creates sustained harmony in our home. Fostering a loving relationship with my wife shows our kids what they should look for in their romantic relationships and sets an example of the respect and appreciation they are to give to the women in their lives, including their mother. In addition, my wife and I parent as a united front and ensure a cohesive parenting style. Undermining each other in front of our children would weaken our authority, so it is essential that parenting is administered in allegiance to each other. My wife is my partner in every sense of the word, and I am grateful to have her as I traverse my life—beyond fatherhood.

I am not sure when it comes to knowing what fatherhood means in all of its truth. I only know what I know, and that knowledge seems to be enough. I can hardly comprehend the love I have for my two boys, and I cannot imagine the amount of sacrifice and dedication that fathers have offered before me. To know what fatherhood means is to know something bigger than me and something that transcends my time here on Earth. My only hope is that my kids will be better men than I was, then be greater fathers than I ever could, and I pray that they will get a little closer to finding out what it truly means to be a father.

Richard Quisenberry

Richard Quisenberry is an educator and John Maxwell certified speaker and trainer. He is passionate about helping students and adults identify and operate in their purpose and reach goals they thought to be unachievable. He has dedicated over 38 years to guiding others to develop talents that lie within themselves, helping them to achieve their goals and dreams, ultimately leading to personal, academic, and professional success.

Richard has achieved a successful career in education since 1983, serving in many capacities, including Principal, District Compliant Coordinator, Crisis Prevention Instructor, Intervention Specialist, Health Teacher, Physical Education, and adaptive physical education, working with students on the Autism Spectrum, Lead Teacher, and Athletic Coach (basketball, football, track).

Richard is a published author of children's stories and inspirational poetry. He is the founder of Golden Recruit Elite Basketball Services, creator of the Wobbly Willie Kindness Program for students (Pre-K through sixth grade), and CEO and founder of Unique Proposals Leadership and transformational life coaching services. In addition, he has been a diligent entrepreneur since creating Quisenberry Enterprise, LLC.

Community outreach and advocacy are essential to Richard. He has served as a facilitator for Christian marriage support groups, helped organize camps for various community programs, worked as a staff member at Ohio Fellowship Christian Church (FCA) summer camps, and is a personal fitness trainer. Richard has also worked at the Clark County Jail teaching leadership principles, and he has most recently created Gentlemen for Life, a mentoring program for young men from seventh grade through college level.

CHAPTER 7

Connecting and Protecting

Richard Quisenberry

Fatherhood has been one of the greatest learning tools in my life. I try to live in such a way that it is safe for all those who I influence to imitate the love and respect that I give to them and other family members. To have a limitless supply of love and support for my wife and children requires a combination of empathetic listening, forgiveness, and honest communication, all of which can lessen the possibility of future problems.

The older I get, the more I cherish the privilege of being a husband and father to my biological children and all the youths who refer to me as "Pops." How I conduct myself daily will serve as a frame of reference for their lives. I believe my fatherhood journey has led to me becoming the best version of myself, which puts me in a position to help others become the best versions of themselves, which is a perspective that will outlive me.

My father's work ethic affected me profoundly in more ways than one. He worked as a custodian at a grocery store from 8:00 p.m. to 4:00 a.m., came home to sleep from 5:00 a.m. to 8:00 a.m., ate, and went to work at St. Raphael's School until 3:00 p.m.—and I don't remember him ever taking a day for vacation. Even though my dad's schedule taught me to work with excellence and discipline, growing up, I did not get to spend time with him the way I wanted. I vowed that when I had children, I would spend more time with them because I missed having enough time with my father.

Not only did my father require us to be respectful to everyone, including adults, but he also taught my siblings and me to work with excellence, no matter the job (that included us working during the summers at our high school, Springfield (Ohio) Catholic Central to help pay our tuition).

Dad checked every task we completed, and if the finish didn't meet his standards, we would have to do it again. Seeing my father constantly work and not have time for anything except quick rest encouraged me to pursue a career in education that would allow me time to spend with my wife and children.

One of my greatest rewards has been having our children want to spend unsolicited time with my wife, Andrea, and me when they really don't have to. The adult conversations we now have are so enjoyable. Ashley is 37, Holley is 35, Bianca is 26, Malik is 24, and Darius is 22. Seeing my children display the value of family with each other is fabulous. Intentionally making plans for regular sibling get-togethers to celebrate each other's accomplishments and giving support in times of difficulty — is fabulous. My wife and I were overwhelmed when we found out our children took time to organize and plan a weekend getaway for just the two of us to celebrate our 30th wedding anniversary. It was well planned and well paid for! We felt it was a wonderful gift and their genuine reflection of the importance of family and marriage.

The landscape of life is ever-changing, as well as the people I love and associate with daily. In order for me to interact and communicate effectively, my empathetic listening and patience are two attributes I must continue to improve.

For me, fatherhood was always feeling the responsibility of making sure everyone's needs were met: food, clothes, and a place to call home. If any of these items were not available to my wife and children, I would feel discontent. I worked two jobs to make sure the bills were paid on time, and that also allowed my wife to stay at home to raise the children. She and I grew up with our mothers not working outside the home, so this was important to both of us. We wanted the children always to feel safe, and there is no better place for that than in their own home. Protection was always one of my greatest concerns, and that worry is even greater since they now live in various parts of the United States. So, each night I pray for a hedge of protection around them, but I also taught them to protect themselves by using their voice.

A lot of youngsters use name-calling to shame and control their friends. A situation happened with my oldest daughter Ashley in elementary school when a classmate called her a "zebra" (in reference to my daughter's biracial ethnicity). Ashley responded by telling the girl that she might be a zebra, but she was definitely a loved zebra who was deeply treasured by her mom and dad. I taught them there is no need for cursing or fighting, but you have to let people know when they cross the line.

I knew as my children got older, I could not be with them everywhere. I knew they would face many uncomfortable situations in which they needed to learn to clarify how they wish to be treated. During many of these occurrences, my children were not happy with me, and I often reminded them my goal was never to do only what they wanted.

Parenting isn't easy, and there are moments when you appreciate your successes but worry about what you consider your failures. I worried when my son Malik felt pressured to get a Division 1 scholarship to play college sports. His older sister and younger brother were rated D-1 athletes, but Malik was not as fortunate. However, as a good athlete, he did receive offers from colleges on the smaller, Division 3 level. I now regret that my actions and language may have made him feel inferior for not achieving the same measure of college athleticism as his siblings.

Malik played college basketball for one year and then decided he would rather pursue other passions. He has found a profound love for music and painting, and he has taught himself to play the piano and different styles of the guitar. He also creates beautiful landscapes and portraits and has sold a few of his artistic works.

A father's words have a great influence on a little boy as he matures into manhood. Unintentionally, I gave Malik the wrong message that obtaining an athletic scholarship was necessary to be successful. This, I considered a failed moment as a father, and it was heartbreaking for me.

Now, since all my children are adults, I was curious about their perception of me, and I asked them to describe me as a father.

Here is the response from my oldest (Ashley):

"My dad was and is a dad full of tough love. As a kid, I never wanted to disappoint him. Disappointing him was the biggest fear I had. There were very few things that would disappoint him, and I stayed as far from them as possible. His career choice allowed him to be very present in our lives. He would show up at school unannounced just to see how we were doing. All our friends loved him. He had a nickname for every friend we had. Our house was the house everyone wanted to be at. In the summers when we were young, we would go wherever he would go — two-a-days when he coached football and different houses when he was painting. From as little as I can remember, I grew up in a gym. We spent many afternoons with mats built up around us like a playpen. Dad would lift weights while my sister and I would read or color."

"I remember going through the drive-through store to get snacks. Sometimes we would have to wait all day, but we better not complain about it. I remember watching his favorite television shows with him,

Bionic Woman, a lot of sci-fi channels, and *Walker Texas Ranger*. At first, I didn't really enjoy the shows, but I think what I enjoyed was spending time with him.

My dad is very comfortable with his emotions. I understand that comes with age, but even as a young child, I remember my dad being very vocal about his love for his family. Most of my dad's lessons stick with me are not what he told us to do. I learned them by watching his actions, and it became innate. A memory that sticks with me was when my dad gave his old car to a good friend of his that did not have one. He always meant what he said, and you never had to worry about him following through on his word."

"As emotional as my dad is, I feel like he never worried about hurting our feelings. He did not need to be our friend, and there was very little sugar coating that went on in our house. He knew we would be fine, and if we weren't, well, I guess we'd get over it. He didn't raise his voice much with me because I didn't need that, but when he did, I could still feel his love coming through those stern words."

"Many lessons were taught through sports or house and yard work. It was always a team effort on Saturday mornings to clean the house. We would turn up some music and get to work. My dad has never believed in sleeping in. He would get up early and work out every morning before school. In the summer or on weekends when we had friends over, he would let us sleep in until about 9. He may give us one chance to wake up, and if we weren't up after that, we would be woken up by pots and pans."

110

Here is the response from the second oldest (Holley):

"When I think of my childhood, it's unquestionable that my dad was one of the biggest influences during that time. What I remember is loving yet stern expectations in perfect balance. As kids, my siblings and I knew that if Dad caught wind of any bad behavior, we would get a 'stern talking to' at home. He knew how to be playful and innovative but working hard remained a priority. To this day, I can still see that reflected in his work ethic because he's always pushing himself to do more, learn more, and develop personal growth. There's no doubt that I get my 'busy body' qualities from him. It's a gift to feel like the sky's the limit, and even more so to see it modeled by someone as influential to a child such as a parent."

My 3rd daughter (Bianca):

A mother completes the pillars of a stable home, while a present father is the foundation on which the home sits. Just as there is nothing like a mother's love, there is nothing like a father's leadership. The leadership my dad has shown in my life has been a beautiful balance of tough love and the perfect reflection of what he asked of us daily.

My mother is one of my best friends in my adult life, but I am a daddy's girl through and through. Our first bond came through basketball.

Now, all of my siblings have played organized basketball at some point, but I was the first child to really take it seriously. The day in middle school I decided I wanted to fully commit to basketball as the main sport, he held me accountable for my choice. Being held accountable meant sacrificing things I wanted to do at the moment for daily deposits awaiting a long-term reward.

After growing up running around basketball gyms because my dad was a coach himself, I now became a "coach's kid." This was the start of understanding the value of your name. Your name will give credibility far before your presence. The goal wasn't to be successful but to give a full effort in all you do in the journey to be successful. This included expecting excellence out of us, not perfection.

A phrase used often by my dad is, "The way we do one thing is the way we do everything. 110%." This not only pertained to inside the lines of the court but in all aspects of life. Growing up consisted of creating the habit of following through on what you said you'd do and doing it with excellence. The kitchen wasn't cleaned completely before bed? You will be woken up in the middle of the night to finish it. Do you want to quit a card game because you're losing? No, you will finish what you started. Do you no longer want to play on a sports team? That is a conversation YOU will conduct with the coach.

The lessons always felt heavy and uncomfortable at the moment, but I never knew the preparation those same lessons provided for adult life. Now that I am older, I am never thankful enough to have had a dad who not only told me the way to do right by others and, more importantly, myself...but to have a dad who has shown me the way by example.

The same man that was asking you to get up at 4:00 AM to work out before high school was the same man already getting up every day at 3:00 AM to read before the workout. The same man that told me he loved me showed me how to love in the way he loves my mom. The same man who demands excellence of me demands excellence of himself, and to have a father like that has been a blessing that will impact generations of this family.

My older son's (Malik) response was short but powerful:

He states, "My father is the most influential individual in my life. My mother has also had a huge impact, but it's different in the sense that she can't teach me how to be a man. My father not only told me what it means to be a man but showed me how through his actions and the way he lives his life. Because of this, I am forever grateful."

My youngest (Darius):

"I don't even know where to start about the father, mentor, and friend that you have been in my life. So, I will go through each one of them. As a father, I wouldn't have made it if I didn't have you as my dad. I would have ended up in jail or in the ground, most likely, because of the routes and things I just naturally got into as a young kid. We laugh about it, but all those *whoopins* really helped me learn right from wrong, not just them alone. It was how you explained to me *why* afterward and that you still loved me even though I may not have wanted to hear it at the time, obviously, but subconsciously I needed it to know that you were doing it out of love and not out of hate for me."

"Just the simple things like separating father and coach. You worked three jobs while mom stayed home to take care of us, and still came home somehow with energy and played with us kids, like 'riding the bull' that we used to do. Even now that I'm older, I understand how much effort that takes after a long day, when all you want to do is lay down and debrief from the day."

"As a mentor, you did the best job of separating coach and father. You pushed me as hard as I wouldn't, and you didn't accept the mediocre out of me. If I would not go hard, I was going to get kicked out of the gym. Not that I wasn't good enough to go with Bianca and Malik, but you knew from your experiences that nothing in life comes easy, and when you saw me wasting my God-given potential, you made me leave until I was ready to work. Also, the life lessons you explained to Malik and me about not being held to the same standard as other kids we were around at Tecumseh (a rural school). We couldn't do or say a lot of certain things because we weren't looked at the same. We didn't get as many chances as some others did. That's why it was so imperative to be respectful and say 'yes, sir' or 'no, sir' when addressing adults."

"Last, you became one of my best friends when I got older, as I am now. I can tell you pretty much anything that goes on in my life. But the most important thing is that I can tell you and not feel judged by the world or you. You listen, regardless of how bad or messed up I may be. You just give me your best advice and let me know you love me and that you are with me, regardless. I don't think you know how much that means to me to have an outlet like you to express certain things going on in my life, too. No matter what it is, you always know the right things to say. I love you, Dad, with everything in me. I know that everything that is coming in the future to you and that lovely woman I get to call my mom and you call your wife because, without you two co-parenting, I would have never made it close to where I am today without you both. It may not have been perfect, especially during my junior year in high school when we went through turmoil together. But what family is perfect, right? It's about the love and desire to never give up on each other, no matter what. That is what you have instilled in all of your kids: Family comes first!"

My wife's response is similar yet different:

She states, "My husband has always taken pride in being a father to our children. He has always taken an active role in their lives ever since they were born: changing diapers, taking turns staying up in the middle of the night, helping around the house, taking and picking them up from school, etc. Nothing was off-limits to him. Together, we made a great team in raising our children."

Connector: As a father of five, one of my greatest aspirations in life is to connect with my children's hearts. To love and discipline them in a manner that is pleasing to God and undeniably loving and respectful to them. Continuously keeping them comfortable with personal growth requests and activities, while always helping navigate them in the direction of becoming the best version of themselves. This is a daily task I've entrusted to myself.

However, connecting with my children is not my ultimate goal in life. Their connection with Jesus Christ is an unparalleled connection that I crave for all my children. This is the legacy I am striving to leave.

Protector: I have always been diligent about physically protecting my children and keeping them safe and out of harm's way. Teaching them to love themselves and their uniqueness is a key to achieving a level of strong mental health. Asking them to protect the Quisenberry name is the gift I asked for on my 61st birthday in 2021. I genuinely believe a family name is more precious than any amount of money or other material items.

Fatherhood and family - man's most cherished gifts to love, connect, and protect.

Mark McClintock

Mark was born and raised in Kingsport, TN. After graduating from high school, Mark attended Austin Peay State University (APSU) in Clarksville, TN, where he played football and met his now-wife of 16 years. After graduating from APSU (Let's go Peay!) with a bachelor's degree in business, Mark later earned an MBA in marketing from American Intercontinental University. Mark now resides in Greater Atlanta with his wife, daughter, and dog and works as a business development professional. You can find Mark on the golf course when he isn't working and spending time with the family. "A Fatherless Curiosity" is Mark's first authorship contribution.

mark.mcclintock80@gmail.com

CHAPTER 8

Figuring Out Fatherhood

With the Help of Father Figures

Mark McClintock

Almost anyone can father a child, but it takes a man to be a dad. The title "Dad" is earned in my eyes. To me, being a dad means you are present in your child's life, provide for them as necessary, and make sure your child knows you love and support them. I despise the fact there are "deadbeat dads" out there because my father has never been a consistent presence in my life. My  father left when I was very young, so I grew up with just my mom raising me. I understand how it feels to be a child that does not feel loved, supported, or provided for by their father. I always wondered why my father wasn't trying to be a part of my life. What was he doing that was so much more important than being there with me? Did I do something wrong to cause him not to be around? What could I do to make him want to spend some time with me? I became disappointed in the man that my father had become, and I vowed I would never be like him no matter what the circumstances were.

As I look back on my childhood, I relived some moments where I feel his love and support should have manifested themselves. My mother raised me as a single parent. Without welfare assistance, my mother would not have been able to make ends meet. I never heard my mom say, "Your dad is going to get your school clothes this year," "Your dad is contributing to food this month," .... or even for this day. I believe men have an obligation to provide at least the basics for their children. Fathers should come up with a financial plan to take care of their children, even if the child is not in their household. My mother should not have struggled. Let me be clear, my mom did an excellent job of raising me. We had little, but she would always make sure that I was well fed, well clothed, and felt loved. I was never without, and I truly appreciate the sacrifices and efforts she made to raise me as a single mom.

But, even with all the love and attention I was being showered with from my mother, I have asked myself over the years what would love from my father have looked like to me as a child? One of my earliest childhood memories was my 10th birthday. At that point, I had not heard from my father for a few years, and he sent me a birthday card. "Wow, he does love me," I thought. He recognized me; he sees me! Just with a $2 card, I felt acknowledged and like I was enough. Then it stopped. Even just being acknowledged for being alive felt good. I thought during that time that all I needed from him was a card every once in a while. Please, just acknowledge that I am yours. Acknowledge that I am alive. I knew I wanted more than just a card in the mail, but I would take what I could get. Love had become, "Just take what you can get." I became numb to him not being there and just accepted this was the way it was going to be.

I played football from elementary school until college. Out of the hundreds of opportunities for my father to support me during practices, scrimmages, and games, he attended one scrimmage. I remember that day because I balled out on the field. It was like I had an extra boost of energy! I would feel envious that other players had their dads cheering them on the sidelines. I remember daydreaming about seeing my father out there wearing my number, hyping me up after the games, smack-talking about me with the other dads. No child should have to daydream about support. Support is free! Thankfully, I had a supportive mom, but I still longed for my dad's presence. I wanted him to be proud of me. But I had to "just take what I could get." I proudly wore his last name on the back of my jersey and vowed that I would figure out a way to bring honor to that name.

Fatherhood is a blessing from God that should be respected. There should be a plan for the father to be present in their child's life, no matter the circumstances. I can speak from firsthand experience that it does matter and can be impactful. Despite my father's absence, I was able to navigate life positively. My daughter, Amora, is the center of my life, and I am a proud father. I did not allow the pain of my father's absence to manifest itself into unnecessary anger and violence in my life. This cycle is over, and I am bringing honor back to our name. I have taken the responsibility and blessing of fatherhood head-on by being present, providing as necessary, and ensuring my child knows I love her.

My father showed me the blueprint of what *not to do* when I became a father myself. My uncles Sonny and Richard provided a very good representation of what being a dad should look like. Not having any siblings to interact with at home, I always spent time at one of my uncle's houses playing with my cousins. They were great at showing love while also being a disciplinarian and seemed always to be present. I learned a lot from my uncles. Each one had different strengths and taught me different lessons. Uncle Sonny is my mother's brother (wife Mary), and Aunt Gina is my mother's sister (husband Richard). What I learned from my uncle Sonny is discipline. He was in the military and ran his house like a drill sergeant. Uncle Sonny had two boys, and I remember when I would stay over, they expected us to do some type of work around the house. Uncle Sonny was into fitness and often challenged us to execute a crazy exercise he discovered during a tour. My uncle Richard was completely different. He is my fun-loving uncle. He was playful and young at heart. We would pass football in front of his house and play video games at night almost every time I visited. He also ran a tight ship but with a more laid-back vibe. I learned the importance of having fun with your children from my uncle Richard. Both uncles were great providers for their families and always made me feel included whenever I was around. Although I'm thankful for the impact my uncles had on my life, I wish I could say my father had a more positive influence during my upbringing. I would be remiss if I didn't say my uncles' spouses, Aunt Mary and Aunt Gina also treated me as one of their own during my frequent cousin visits. If I wasn't at home, which was most of the time, I was consistently in one of their households. It wasn't always sunshine and rainbows during these visits. I was disciplined and taught life lessons like I was one of their children. I'm appreciative now because it helped shaped me into the man I am today.

I wish I could say that I grew up as a "spoiled" only child. My mom did everything she could to provide, and I was never without; however, not having an additional provider in the house caused struggles. We lived in public housing and relied on welfare assistance. We barely had a dependable car. I was my babysitter when my mom had to work if I wasn't spending the night at one of my uncle's houses. It is amazing to think back on birthdays and Christmas and how my mom would almost always find a way to get me that gift I really wanted. I unconsciously made mental notes about what I would do to be a great provider for my future family. I figured out a way to channel what could have been "woe is me" energy into a desire to be better than he was as a father and as a man. I was determined to make him proud of me and what I would accomplish without his help or guidance. My father's absence ignited an achieving attitude within me, and with God's favor shining down on me, I did just that. I graduated from high school with honors and was the first in my family to attend and graduate from college. During my junior and senior years, I was a team captain on my college football team. I later obtained my MBA with honors. I've since had a very successful career in sales and feel like I'm just getting started. The latter achievements were to not only advance in my career but also to set a good example and provide for my daughter. My hope is that Amora will do even bigger and better things in life than I have, not despite me, but from being motivated and inspired by my efforts.

There are way too many selfish "parents" in this world who prioritize other things over being present in their children's lives. I trust Amora sees and appreciates the effort that her mother and I both make to be present in her life and won't take what she has for granted. Leveraging my father's greatest impact of not being present into positivity, I vowed to experience my child's first steps, first words, and all the first experiences he or she would have while growing up. It was very important to me to ensure that my child felt loved and recognized that I wanted the best for them because I didn't have that assurance in my life from my father. My desire is that Amora positively receive the impact I am striving to make in her life. I cannot say that I wouldn't wish what I went through growing up on anybody because it was and continues to be character-building for me. I would hope that any child going through life without their father finds reliable father figures as I did. I pray they can channel any hurt and pain from that void into ambition, goals, and a hunger for achievement also as I have. Do I wish my father stayed in my life? Of course, I do! However, I now embrace my past and his decisions because it taught me what I needed to do not to make the same mistakes. I'm not a perfect man or parent by any means, but I know that I'm at least giving my best effort to do what is right for my family.

My greatest reward for being a father is also the most painful part of being a dad. Watching your little one transition from an infant to a toddler to a pre-teen and now a teenager is one of the coolest things I've experienced in my life. The time goes by way too fast, however. I implore you, fathers, to be as present as possible for your child, especially during the years of one through five. That is the only timeframe when they are still truly "babies," and just about every experience is new to them. It is so much fun and chaotic at times to witness. You know how it feels when you visit a family member or friend shortly after they have had a child. Then you make a return visit in what seems no time at all, and that child is a completely different person. They are almost unrecognizable because they have changed so much! Watching your child grow up firsthand and witnessing all those changes is remarkable. Social media and various apps that provide photo reminders do not make going through this process any easier. I love (sarcasm) those random reminders of pictures I took of our daughter three, five, or nine years ago. These alerts have literally brought me to tears on more than one occasion seeing the sweet little girl our daughter Amora once was. She is still sweet but not at all little these days.

Being able to impart life lessons I learned while growing up to my daughter is also rewarding. Our goal as parents should be to help our children avoid the mistakes we might have made growing up. It's important to let our kids live freely and experience the ups and downs of life because that is how we all learn. But when I can provide guidance that will help Amora eliminate any major pitfalls, I do. I also love trying to make our daughter challenge herself to see what it feels like to accomplish something she may have thought she couldn't. There are learning opportunities even during times when she doesn't achieve a goal. I think it's good for her to have those moments as well to understand that life does not always go how you want it to. Even in those instances, however, the direction is that with more hard work, she can attain her desired outcome. And that goes for anything she sets her mind to.

I get an overwhelming sense of satisfaction just being present in various family moments. From time to time, I'll look around and just think, "wow, I surely had nothing like this growing up." Just being a part of a consistent family unit is a blessing. I try to act tough or like I don't want to do some things my daughter asks me to do with or for her. But on the inside, I'm pumped! Amora wanting us to keep up with an anime series we started, going to get ice cream together to satisfy a sugar fix, or taking her to the bookstore to buy new books. These are moments I enjoy spending with her. Speaking of books, I love how much she loves to read! Most of her allowance or whenever she gets a hold of any money is spent on books. When Amora was two years old, I started making her read her bedtime stories to me. It was painfully cute sounding our way through words at first, but she soon grasped how words and sentencing worked and became a super reader by the age of three. She reads way more than I did growing up and will read a ton more than I will in my lifetime. It is rewarding to know that I helped create that love for story, adventure, and learning within her.

Knowing what I know now and how fast time goes by, if I could do anything differently as a young father, I would go back to relive when Amora was growing up between the ages of one through five. I appreciate every single experience, and I don't believe that I was neglectful at all, but I selfishly think I could have squeezed in even more father-daughter moments between us. After she turned four, I would have kept picking her up instead of saying, "You're a big girl now; let's walk." We would go to even more games and events together. I would have recorded almost every encounter in the memory bank of that special age range. Actually, I think having more footage and photos to be reminded of that ridiculously cute age timeframe would make knowing that my little girl is growing up even worse.

In all seriousness, there isn't much I would change other than ensuring I was as present as I felt like I was for my daughter. I might have tried to conduct more candid conversations about how things made her feel and why to help her understand my response to certain things. I would ensure that even in discipline, she knew my actions were coming from a place of love, care, and concern for her. The most important thing for me would be confirmation that she knows how much I love her. Even before I became a father, I promised myself that I would be a dad to my child. Being worthy of the "daddy" moniker by Amora is an amazing feeling.

My two pieces of advice for young fathers, both I consider critical, are: 1) Do everything you can to be present in your child's life, and 2) be patient with them. With all the disruptions and distractions that occur in life (*and only accumulate as you get older*), being present and patient helps you build a solid bond with your little one.

Whether you are still in a relationship with the mother of your child or not, make a concerted effort just to be there consistently. Your presence means so much to your son and daughter, especially early on. As they grow older, the expectation becomes for you to be present and accessible, which is a great thing! If you can't be present in your child's life consistently, you must have a good reason, and there absolutely has to be communication on why you are absent. If there's a will, there is a way, so you'll be hard-pressed to come up with legitimate excuses on why you can't be present. As I mentioned, my mother and father divorced very early in my childhood, and my father didn't consider being present in my upbringing to be a priority. I have the fortune and favor to still be married to my wife and mother of our daughter, going on 16 years strong. Being in the same household makes it a lot easier for me to be present in our daughter Amora's life. With work and other social obligations, it can get a little tricky to be vigilant in my efforts to be present for my daughter. Just being in the same house doesn't always mean being accessible, so I try to be mindful of making sure she knows that I'm there for her. As your little one transitions into a teen, it can sometimes seem that they are growing away from you. I do everything I can to show affection to Amora, so she knows that my love is and always will be there for her.

Practice patience. Remember, they are kids, and most of the time will need to make mistakes to learn what not to do. Even after being told why they should or should not be doing something, learning the why in real life can be more impactful. It can seem that your child is testing your patience, and they may very well be doing that now and then, but it's just inexperience. Try to always show love to your daughter or son. Even when you don't think they are paying attention, they are absorbing your actions and reactions. It's amazing to see how your traits come out of this little being you helped create. It won't always be easy to express patience with your child, but do your best to be mindful of how you react. Patience doesn't mean don't discipline. I try to set expectations for chores, responsibilities, etc. for Amora and remind her when she fails to meet them. The goal is to raise our child into a responsible adult. I believe instilling some level of discipline will help her grow into an accountable person in life. She is much more privileged than I was growing up, so I'm praying that these things will stick with her.

Time flies, so be sure to appreciate the innocence of your child's youth. It is amazing how fast your child goes from this tiny little thing to a full-on adolescent that's about to enter high school! Watching my daughter Amora's personality develop and change over time has been exciting, funny, and sad all at the same time. She went from being my golf buddy to hesitantly wanting to hang around with me and her mom as much as a teenager, especially in public, in what seems like a blink of an eye. We understand what she is going through, but we also take every chance we can get to embarrass her with our love. We have no shame at all with that. I'm sure she will appreciate it one day. Not so much at the moment, though. But through it all, I just try to remain present and patient with her. Teen patience is very different from little girl's or toddler patience, however. That's a whole other chapter. There are worse things in this world, so I wouldn't change it for anything. I love my not-so-little girl!

As a new father, if you feel lost or don't know where to start, talk to someone you consider a great father to their children. The truth is, most of us don't know what we are doing at first, but we learn and figure it out by trial and error. The most important thing you can do is to stick around and try.

Troy Cromer

Troy was born and raised in Sandusky, Ohio, a town positioned west of Cleveland and east of Toledo on Lake Erie. He was the last child of three born to his beloved late parents, Thomas Jr. and Mable Cromer. As a youngster, he participated in sports and church activities like most of his friends in the community.

After high school, Troy moved to Columbus, Ohio and attended DeVry Institute of Technology, as it was once called, and later attended Ohio State University. Soon after transferring to Ohio State, Troy's first child, a son, Terrance was born. He dropped out of college to pursue full-time employment. Five years later, his daughter Abrianna was born and Troy returned to Sandusky to work in manufacturing at Ford Motor Company.

During his time at Ford, Troy persevered and matured through the challenges of fatherhood and full-time employment to provide a good lifestyle for his children. He was employed by Ford for 12 years until the auto industry crashed, forcing him to end his tenure.

Troy would later move to the Atlanta area and marry the mother of his daughter Natalie. He enjoys the easy winters in Georgia and continues working in manufacturing as a supervisor.

CHAPTER 9

If You Wake Up, You Still Have an Opportunity

Troy Cromer

Fatherhood provides the opportunity to serve your family and others through acts of love, leadership, provision, knowledge, and inspiration. The complexity of fatherhood travels through time, touching the lives of those who are divinely intended to have an influence over the fruit they are blessed to have. Fatherhood has a very subtle beginning, but the future solely depends on the individual it has been granted. He will have the privilege of guiding and teaching a child how to communicate, resolve problems, and learn about life's responsibilities and important experiences.

I will admit that I have a better understanding of fatherhood now that I am older and don't have any babies to raise. But, as a young father, I did not have a clear mind to carry out the responsibilities successfully. Today, I know how special fatherhood is, and I can reflect on the past and see where mistakes were made. Even though I can describe it using broad terms, the full depth of fatherhood cannot be thoroughly expressed by the mere stroke of a pen or in a single written chapter. Now, I realize that.

Lessons From My Father

How could I discuss my fatherhood experience without first acknowledging the influence of my father? I simply could not. He is my beginning. There is no way I could accurately convey my father's total impact on my life, for he gave my siblings and me so much. Let me be clear and declare that we were never rich or well-off. Instead, the wealth of my father's presence in our lives takes the forefront. As an adult, I can appreciate his directions and guidance. I cherish and remember my father's character, personality, physical appearance, strength, and knowledge. The effect those qualities had on me is priceless. He provided me with a sense of determination through the noble and commendable deeds he has done. He has given me examples of how to handle conditions that, at times, may not be favorable for me. He passed to my siblings, myself, and others the lessons on how to love in personal relationships we would encounter throughout our lives. His teachings have been invaluable.

His work ethic is something I still admire today. He worked for Ford Motor Company for 36 years. He began working there before I was born as an assembly person and eventually worked his way to Superintendent. Throughout his years working for Ford, my father worked even harder for several businesses, including a food takeout business, as a partner in a construction company, and for a flourishing real estate business where he owned multiple properties. While managing his various responsibilities may have been challenging,

Dad never seemed to lose. As a kid growing up, watching his drive and strong work ethic right before my eyes gave me a sense of pride.

I was proud of my dad for all he did to provide a pleasant living for our family.

I watched my father's relationships and how he interacted with others. Some were his closest and dearest friends. Others he respected highly but held to a slightly different level of association. Even observing his relationship with my mom, his wife, was a valuable learning experience. During my teen years, Mom and Dad were not as emotionally attached as they once were. Although their marriage was estranged, they did what they could to remain cordial and civil while raising us throughout their time in the same household. Even throughout this time, my dad remained a good, stand-up father. I learned that even if you and the woman you have a family with are not getting along, there is still the obligation to fulfill as a father. You still have to show up when needed and provide for your family. Every time you open your eyes, you have an opportunity to make something good happen. He often said, "When you wake up, you have a decision to make. You can either be a part of the problem or part of the solution. Now, pick a side."

I have always tried to convey this principle to my kids - *make good decisions, and the outcomes will more likely be in your favor.* I hope they have seen enough to learn from my experiences and won't repeat my mistakes.

A Student in Father's Shoes

When my son was born, I was a young man two and a half years after graduating high school, still trying to finish college.

When I learned I was about to take on a big responsibility, I had to decide how to navigate a space that was not previously defined for me. I had ideas but no complete understanding of what it would take to create a successful life and do what was in the best interest of my child. I only knew how to be who I had been for the first 20 years - a son, brother, nephew, and cousin. I had witnessed my older siblings' relationships, but it's completely different when it's your situation.

I had to navigate a relationship with a young mother-to-be in her final year of high school. Because we were so young, we often clashed about how to proceed in the relationship. Our foundations were different. I grew up comfortably at home with both my parents, husband and wife. She grew up with her mother. Her father was not in the same household. As it turned out, she had some struggles with her father. I loved her, but I did not realize her relationship with her dad would become a problem for us, nor did I foresee it affecting our roles as new parents. I knew I had strong feelings for her, and we were about to become first-time parents.

While waiting for my son to be born, I attended college and worked part-time, two hours away. She began to attend college as her womb grew. Phone calls were our primary communication source, but I often spent weekends with her. As I look back, I realize those weekends together were likely the source of friction between us. The times I wasn't there may have caused her to feel a certain way, possibly even thinking I would turn out like her father - absent from our child's life. But I was focused on getting through college so everything would turn out well for all of us.

Although I was two hours away at a Division 1 university in the state capitol, I didn't date others while I was in a relationship with her. Indeed, there was plenty of temptation around me. But I was able to get through it all fairly well. It wasn't until a year after my son was born that we began to have communication problems, and the dreaded *baby mama drama* started to thrust its ugly head into my life.

We would have spats about our relationship, or lack thereof. It seemed, at times, as if she would not allow me to spend time with our son. The closeness that we once shared was deteriorating, and 'the blues' about us began. Then came the frustration, arguments, anguish, lies, and partial truths. In the meantime, we still had to do whatever was in the best interest of our child. During this period, life felt so defeating. It seemed like my life and heart were being ripped apart right before my eyes. My feelings for her were still strong, but how I was treated made life problematic for me.

Eventually, I would get input from my parents and a couple of friends. The 'Crew,' my male friends from childhood, would always say, "Stop being so wrapped up in a girl who is mistreating you so much." My dad would repeat the same thing and say, "You're gonna self-destruct, worrying about some girl." But my mother's words were the most impressionable. Momma said, "If a woman wants something, a woman is gonna do something. In other words, a woman will go after what she wants, and if she doesn't go after it, she doesn't want it." So, it would be in my best interest to go on through life without her. But that meant going on without her, not without my child. After a year or so, I was able to move on. The baby mama drama continued, but deciding to move on without her was no longer an issue. Little did I know this initial experience would help me get through the birth of my second child.

A New Experience

I began dating other women. One particular woman, Liz, came into my life and showed me more than I could ever imagine. We worked for the same banking company but in different departments. The first time I met Liz, we were dating other people. The woman I was dating, let's call her Ava, also worked for the same company. Forever the hopeless romantic, I thought we would be together for a long time. But, no. Ava was a girl from the city, and I was just a small-town guy. About a year into dating Ava, our relationship started to decline. Soon after, she was pregnant, but the child was with some other guy. I felt she was seeing others behind my back the entire time we dated, but I never thought she'd get pregnant.

Nevertheless, our time together ended. Ending the relationship with Ava was not as destructive or devastating as my previous relationship.

Liz came into my life, rather surprisingly to her. I actually saw Liz before I met Ava. I had attended college with the guy she was dating, so I knew of her, but only in passing. I would see Liz in different hangouts, and we even shared a few common interests, unbeknown to her. Life can be funny sometimes, and one of those times came when Ava was having a birthday party. As I mentioned, we all worked for the same company. In the early 90s, February to be exact, Ava invited a few people from the company to her birthday celebration, including me, even though we were done. Liz was also at the party, but she didn't know I knew her. I didn't think it would be a suitable time to pursue Liz because of Ava's family's presence. But the following September, a common friend invited both of us to his party. This was the right time for me to pursue her.

We exchanged numbers and started seeing each other. Some time passed, and one cold winter day, Liz told me she was having my second child and her first. Though I was slightly surprised, I did not shy away from what would happen in the coming months.

My life was evolving, and changes were being made. I was no longer a full-time student and part-time worker. I was a full-time worker and a part-time student. I found it necessary to make changes for my son. It was difficult, but it had to be done. He needed clothes, formula, health insurance, shoes, and much more. His mom worked, but I had a responsibility. And now, with my second child on the way, I had to make more changes and prepare to bring another life into the world.

My tie to Liz differed from the other two women before her. Liz and I had love and respect for one another. Her background, as I found out later, was even more diverse. She grew up between two different landscapes, the mountains of West Virginia and Ohio. She had a foundation of religion and structure. She was an independent single woman who had been living on her own since she was 18. She was grown. I grew fond of her rather quickly, but we would go through our share of problems as things would have it. Now *baby mama drama* was just a typical day in life, and no day was ever safe from its presence. It will pop up any day of the week when you are an unmarried parent.

When my daughter was born, we both took a stance on being present for her. We were on the same page concerning our roles and responsibilities. We understood parenting responsibilities better. Me, from my previous experiences, and Liz, from the values her family instilled in her. Despite our bond losing strength, we ensured our responsibilities and respect remained integral to our relationship. Even when we officially separated, that never changed. Not to say our relationship was perfect, but it was never in a place of serious disarray.

I followed the routine of setting up visits. I made sure my support order was intact and not behind. I bought whatever items were needed. I was an official father of two and had to do whatever was good for my children, even if it meant more sacrifice. My kids will know their father was present and always tried to do good for them.

I would bring them together as often as possible, even though they lived two hours apart. They knew and loved each other. They would play together and even disagree, as normal siblings do. We would go on trips and outings together. If something was going on with one of them and the other didn't know, I'd be sure to tell them about what was happening in their sibling's life. These were challenging times, but it had to be done.

I would be remiss if I did not mention that the honor and respect Liz and I shared, and still share, was fully manifested one sunny day in May when she honored me by becoming my wife!

A Lasting Connection

The connection I have with my children is the reward I cannot get enough of. Growing up in the 70s and 80s differed vastly from today. I am sure that each generation has its uniqueness, so the constant factor of change should not be a surprise. But, in the initial phase of my fatherhood journey, I imagined that raising my children would repeat how I was raised.

After all, my childhood experiences were my example, my playbook to follow. Even if I did not have the precise know-how, I had a model to pattern my journey after.

But there were differences. I established a more open forum for communication with my children versus how my father and I communicated. My father was a leader in every sense of the word. His word was the law, and there was little room for discussion or debate. That does not mean he was an insensitive dictator. Instead, he needed to lead his household in a certain way.

I was raised with discipline being first on the list during my adolescent years. Because of that, I also prioritized discipline for my children. However, I honestly believe it was not the level of discipline that I had experienced. I'll admit it. My kids can attest to that fact as well. As a result, my kids are more apt to talk through tough subjects with me and not feel intimidated because of a crushing disciplinary action that may ensue.

I believe it comes down to the "3 Ps" in life - positivity, poise, and persistence. The 3 Ps was something my late high school football coach instilled in our team, and, as grown men, we still bring up that phrase in our conversations today. These principles would help guide me through some of the trials of fatherhood when dealing with my children.

I knew my children would need to be cared for physically, emotionally, and financially. One thing I did not do as a young father was fail them financially. Let's be clear, I am not a well-off or rich man financially, but I never allowed my financial obligations to be a burden for me. Sure, as a young man, I was often tempted by the thought of not paying child support if I could get away with it, as some did. But I did not go through with it. During those times, my children's needs and the court's order to pay support were enough for me to do just that. On the other end of my thinking was the shame I would feel if I were ever known as a deadbeat dad or a loser. I remember going into the Post Office years ago and seeing pictures and descriptions of delinquent fathers on display at the front counter - FOR ALL TO SEE. You could see that 'so-and-so' was behind in paying child support and how much they were behind. I remember thinking, what a terrible thing to be posted in this governmental display showing your total arrears. No way would I owe someone a house or a significant amount of money because I refused to do what was good for my kids. Some of the amounts were that large. During those times (the early 80s), if you owed $30,000, it was enough to buy a house.

My kids knew of the court orders, and they knew I paid faithfully. They weren't aware in elementary school, but I am sure they knew as teenagers. But it all plays a part in how they see me. They knew then and now that I am a man who lives his life with integrity, honesty, and nobility.

If I Could Do it Over Again

There is no book written that can truly tell you how to be a father. Every child is different, and every father is different. There is no one-size-fits-all prescription or formula. It is a learning and growing process with every child during each stage of their lives. With that said, I have made my share of mistakes, especially as a young father. If I could have a re-do, I would have more difficult conversations about expectations of the roles in a family structure. As a young man, too often, I relied on a gut feeling or an impulse to drive my actions in deciding what to do next. Now that I am older and wiser, I realize the importance of conveying expectations and goals early and often. My idea is to lessen the blow of the *baby mama drama*.

Mothers and fathers differ, and disagreements or discord will occur because of those very differences. But it does not mean we cannot accomplish what is necessary for the good of our children. As young people, we don't always keep our emotions in check to make the best decision. If we would, instead, take the time to have a conversation about the situation, we would likely be better off. Leading with our emotions takes us in a direction we may regret later. This was my experience many times.

To all young single fathers, I say - talk more. Be bold and brave enough to have difficult conversations with the young lady who will have your child. Take the time to eliminate misunderstandings and prevent harmful and disruptive consequences that may cause irreparable damage to a coveted, valuable relationship. Do what you can to prepare your mind for disagreements. Remember, no two minds are alike, so you will have disagreements.

Be ready and prepared to compromise or make a sacrifice. Although you may want the most favorable outcome of a situation concerning your child, try to be prepared for the unexpected result that may not be in your favor. You will have to, more than likely, compromise. There is no way to accurately predict the outcome because you have to consider the child and the mother. But at least you will be prepared.

So, with that, I say: be sure your wife wants to have a child. Purposely I say "wife." I have learned there is no match between two people working together versus one on their own. The difficulties of life can be a seriously heavy burden to carry. It is much easier to experience fatherhood with someone who can be trusted and respected and who will share some of the responsibilities with you.

"Who can find a virtuous and capable wife?
She is more precious than rubies."
~ Proverbs 31:10 NLT

Show Love - Early and Often

While I tried to show my children love and affection, I recognize that I could have conveyed it to them more often. But showing love and affection are areas that always have an opportunity to grow.

My kids and I shared outings and travels, and I pray those memories will stay in their hearts. But the primal need for love that we all have can't be expressed enough.

To the young fathers trying to get through a time where you don't know all the answers and don't have a father or mentor to turn to, don't get caught into the mindset that you always need to pound your chest or fists to prove you are a man. Begin while your children are infants, small precious creations, to give them love, affection, and attention. Take as much time as possible to hug and talk with them regularly. Get to know all of their little and unique movements. Get to know even their scent.

Do what you can to stay present in their day-to-day activities. Help them learn new things and how to conquer new levels of understanding.

Discover new things with them. Make sure the directions, instructions, advice, suggestions, and lessons will lead them on a good, positive path for a bright future.

It is of the highest importance that you take this action as soon as they are born and follow up on it as frequently as you can throughout their lives. For it won't be long before they are no longer kids. They will become the fruits of your efforts. If you have taken the time to plant, water, and nurture the seeds, good fruit will be the result, and blessings will continue to flow for your children and their children.

Keep in mind that the period of adolescence will fly by faster than you would expect. You may not see it so much through your eyes but just watch. Think about someone you remember as a kid who is an adult now, and I'm sure you will get what I am saying. Often I will ask a child if they are ready for college. Even if they are not in high school yet, I will ask them. Then I go on further to say - "Because you graduate tomorrow." The expressions and reactions I get are funny sometimes because we both know it isn't *tomorrow* yet.

But what I understand, and the little one doesn't understand yet, is how time goes by faster than we can imagine or even understand. It's true that "time waits for no one." Once it's gone, there is nothing you can do about it. It's gone.

Fathers, take the physical and emotional time to show, give, feel, and teach love.

Real Dads Show Up

With all the breakups and separations I experienced in my younger years, there was constantly the need to rebound from a failed attempt. There was always a hurdle to get over or some obstacle in the way. It is rarely easy to maneuver through this course of fatherhood and remain unscathed. The bumps and bruises can sometimes be overwhelming. But, as a father, I still had to show up for my kids. I still had to perform at a high level for them. I still needed to give them an excellent model to view. And you, my brother, will need to do the same.

"3 Ps" - My Legacy

My hope is my children have seen in me great presence, patience, and perseverance. I pray they have taken the good teachings into their hearts and minds and will use those lessons for the greater good of this world to enrich their lives, as well as the lives of others.

"Children are a gift from the Lord; they are a reward from Him. Children born to a young man are like arrows in a warrior's hands. How joyful is the man whose quiver is full of them! He will not be put to shame when he confronts his accusers at the city gates."
~ Psalms 127:3-5 NLT

Micheal Dorris

Micheal Dorris, a twin to sister Michelle, boasts proudly of being the better half of the two. But, he quickly jokes that's the story, as long as he's telling it. Raised in Marietta, Georgia, Micheal and Michelle were born to Josephine and Eddie Ray Dorris. He gives full credit to his parents for their influence on him as a father and for how he raised his children.

Ten years after their high school graduation, Micheal married his sweetheart, Barbara Reid-Dorris, whom he affectionately calls his *little Jamaican firecracker*. A fatherhood mindset began for Micheal long before his children were born. Before Barbara became pregnant, they thought long and hard about being parents, even down to what their children's names should be, considering the struggles of young people of color who are judged based on gender and race. According to Barbara, Micheal had two opportunities to have children; whether they were girls, boys, or a combination of both, there would only be two. And so it was. Micheal is the proud father of two girls, Alex and Taylor Reid-Dorris. Within these pages, Micheal looks at his role as a father, its challenges, and its rewards.

MichealDorris@live.com

CHAPTER 10

Transformation Through Fatherhood

Micheal Dorris

Fatherhood means taking care of my family and putting their needs and safety first. It warrants sacrifices to maintain a stable environment for them. Looking back, I recall the life lessons that have both laid the foundation and given me the fortitude for my journey through fatherhood.

If my father taught me one thing, it was to have a good work ethic. I did not have a curfew when growing up, so I could stay up or out as long as I wanted to on a Friday night, but when the sun rose on Saturday morning, I was expected to be up and ready to help my father to do some physically hard work. I did not know it then, but he was teaching me that when I have an obligation, I have to do whatever it takes to meet that obligation. No excuses. On Saturday mornings, I helped my father with brick mason work - pouring concrete, laying bricks, and even loading railroad ties. For me, this was back-breaking work with lots of heavy lifting. It was not easy, but I earned my pocket money from this work. My father never gave me anything without me earning it, so I learned at an early age if I wanted anything in life, I had to work for it.

My father did not push me to go to college. Instead, he ensured I knew how to make a living with my hands. After high school, I became a certified welder and worked in the Local Iron Workers Union in Atlanta. That career did not last long. I wanted to work for myself, so I started my business which allowed me to be financially independent. It was harder than working for someone, but the money was much better, and because of the work ethic instilled in me when I was young, I knew I had what it took to be successful.

Working for myself came with very long hours, and the stress was sometimes unbearable, but my father taught me I must work hard to get what I want, so that is what I was doing.

Before I became a father, I was impatient with people and myself. I was even impatient with time. I sought instant gratification because who had time to wait?! My actions were never in consideration of how others would be affected. If they couldn't roll with me at my speed, to hell with them. I would keep moving. If I wanted to spend all my money on one thing that served a purpose for that moment, I did. It was simple. I wanted it. I got it. Done. I worked hard so I could spend my money doing whatever I wanted to do. After all, the point of working hard and making money is to spend it, right? My finances did not consider my future (or anyone else's, for that matter). My only responsibility was unto myself.

When I found out I was to be a father, I knew my work-life had to change. My obligations were to my wife and children, so I had to find a balance between work and home. Until my wife, Barbara, was pregnant with our first daughter, I worked as an independent contractor in construction. It was physically taxing and stressful and often required consecutive days on the road. I had an opportunity to work locally, so I jumped at the chance to work a Monday through Friday job. It was a steady job, but the change was a financial sacrifice because the money was not as forthcoming as working for myself. The trade-off was less stress and being home at the end of a regular workday, which was well worth it. I was excited about being able to spend time at home with the children, as I did not want to miss them growing up. Being there for them was important to me because I wanted them to feel and be safe.

When our first daughter, Taylor, was born, we were excited. I was 30 years old, my wife was almost 29, and this was all new to us. I would not be truthful if I said we were not scared. We were both scared sitting in Kennestone Hospital Labor and Delivery room, wondering if the nurses were really going to allow us to take her home. Barbara rode in the back with our first miracle and insisted I drive home at the minimum speed limit for fear of causing any type of injury to the little bundle in the car seat behind me. All the way home, I thought, "Man, I am one lucky guy. I am bringing home my very first baby girl and her mother, and they are both healthy. I'm so blessed that everything turned out as I had hoped."

My last daughter, Alex, arrived 18 months after Taylor was born. She was larger than the doctors predicted, so during birth, there were complications that warranted a crash cart, several emergency personnel, one determined obstetrician, and some much-needed prayers. Initially, I was unsure about the cause of the emergency. Worriedly, I watched as doctors and nurses suddenly crowded my wife's bedside as her obstetrician quickly pushed away her chair at the foot of the bed and got down on her knees to pull at what I could only imagine was my baby. The phone in the room rang. My mother-in-law was on duty in another wing of the hospital. She heard the emergency call on the PA to Labor and Delivery and wondered if everything was OK. I had to tell her, "No." She, her sister, and other co-workers went into a break room and began praying for my wife and new baby girl. As a father, I felt helpless. I could not jump in and help. I did not even know what questions to ask the doctors. I could only sit and watch the frantic actions of the doctors and nurses. I am supposed to be the protector of my wife and children, and all I could do was pray. So, I did. I said a prayer asking God to please let everything be all right. I told Him I wanted to take home another healthy baby, as she will be my last baby, and that I did not want only to take home my baby, but I also wanted to take home my wife, my children's mother, my 'One and Only' because I cannot and do not want to do this alone. I told Him this was my second miracle, and I wanted to teach and watch her learn and experience new discoveries with her big sister, Taylor.

Because of the baby's size, she was stuck in the birth canal and could not get oxygen, and it was too late for an emergency C-section. The doctors' goal was to get her out far enough to suction her nose and get oxygen to her. They succeeded, and when she was finally pulled free, she was gray from the lack of oxygen. My prayers were answered. Thankfully, my baby only suffered a fractured arm which healed on its own. Alex was born weighing in at 10 pounds, 12 ounces, two pounds larger than her sister. At my wife's one-week wellness check with the obstetrician, the doctor told us that if my wife gets pregnant again, the chance of having an even bigger baby was very high. My wife fired a look at me and said she is not having another baby and she will not have any more doctors poking and prodding her after the experience she just endured. I knew what that meant. I had a vasectomy shortly thereafter.

When Taylor and Alex were born, everything changed. As babies and toddlers, I had to be on their schedule. There was no hurrying when I was teaching them to ride a bike or teaching them anything because they learned at their own pace. They dictated when I went to sleep, woke up, and ate meals. As they became teenagers, I had to make my schedule accommodate theirs, so going on vacation was no longer spontaneous and without thought. I had to consider their school breaks and where we would go to ensure they had a good time. My life was no longer on my time, it was all theirs. I had to learn to be patient and considerate.

I also learned to be financially disciplined. Large purchases had to be curtailed because I now had to consider their future. The first large purchase made after Taylor was born was a house. Barbara and I did not want them raised in an apartment because we wanted them to have their own space to run and play and to call their own. Buying a house required discipline in saving for a down payment and other expenses that came with being homeowners. When purchasing the house, I had to consider schools in the area, crime, and traffic, none of which I had given consideration to in the past. My children were now the reason I got up and went to work each day.

Perhaps if my children were boys, I would have taught my sons the same lessons in the same manner my father taught me about work. However, my children are girls, and I did not want my daughters to work physically hard to get what they want. I wanted them to go to college and earn a degree in something that would allow them to earn a good living without doing the back-breaking work I have done. A good work ethic, regardless of what type of job Taylor and Alex chose, was very important, and I worked hard at ensuring that message was conveyed to them long before they were old enough to hold a job.

I have always given my daughters two pieces of advice: First, do NOT get pregnant as a single young woman because that is a hard road to travel. My wife and I had our firstborn 18 months after we were married, so we were not worried about our daughters getting pregnant before getting married because we not only told them, we *showed* them. I told them to live their lives without encumbrances. Learn who they are before getting married or having children. Live independently of anyone before committing to someone, whether husband or child. That's where my second advice came in; get your own shit. That is exactly how my father delivered the advice to me, and that is how I passed it on to my daughters. 'Get your own shit' simply means they are not to depend on nor expect anyone to provide their needs and happiness for them. I did not want them going through life with the mindset that they needed a man to survive.

When Taylor and Alex were younger, they always came to me with questions and possible solutions instead of going to Barbara. If ever I had to direct Taylor and Alex to her for any discussions, announcements, opinions, or advice, they would give me the look that said, "…but we will never hear the end, Daddy." Yes, I'd give that look too. While Barbara went on and on about any subject at hand, the girls and I would secretly glance at each other and get prepared for her to stop, then start again, sometimes days later. So, understandably, they came to me to avoid the lectures.

One of my worst fears was realized, twice. Alex and Taylor got pregnant within 12 months of each other (I think they were trying to kill me). I was heartbroken. I'm not sure if my heart was broken for them and the lifelong commitment they just made or if my ego was bruised because my little girls did not heed my advice. They were always so quick to come to me instead of their mother with challenges in their personal lives. Why didn't I see this coming?

Despite the threat of being lectured, when they each got pregnant, they told their mother first, who then relayed the information to me. My girls feared disappointing me. They both knew I had very high expectations of them, and them becoming mothers was not a part of the plan I had in mind. I initially thought their poor decisions were because of something I lacked in showing them as a father. I thought perhaps I did not give them the confidence they needed to steer clear of peer pressure. I felt like a failure.

They both remembered me telling them that if they should get pregnant, they would have to move out and live as the adults they apparently wanted to be. Soon after having Parker, Alex moved out. Then back in. Then out again. Her mother and I watched her struggle and constantly reminded her she did not have to leave until she was financially ready to live on her own. She said she remembered Daddy telling her and Taylor that if they got pregnant, they had to leave, so she was determined to be on her own. I had no choice but to respect her decision. Taylor soon moved out as well.

I soon came to realize that although I did my best with my daughters, I could not stop them from making their own decisions. Their decisions did not change who they were, my daughters, of whom I will always be proud. My job as a father was to continue to show them unconditional love and hope they will do the same for their boys because that is what I have shown them. I realized that I cannot pre-plan their lives for them, for it is theirs to live.

Taylor's son is now 2 years old, his name is Richard, and Alex's son Parker is 3. These boys have been two of the biggest blessings in my life, and I cannot imagine life without them. I didn't think I could love them as much as I love my daughters, but I do. I feel so lucky to know them and be a part of their lives. They bring me pure joy, and they have two amazing mothers. Watching Alex and Taylor with their children makes me swell with pride. This whole thing could have gone 'sideways' if I allowed my broken heart or ego to get in the way of being the father they needed just when they needed me the most.

The bright side to all of this is knowing that I met two of my grandchildren while I am still young enough to teach, guide, and positively influence them. I look forward to their visits with me, doing the same things I did with their mothers when they were small. Taylor used to fall asleep on my shoulders while I mowed the lawn, and now, Parker climbs on my shoulders while I mow the lawn. They, too, are my pride and joy.

My daughters' successes in their personal goals have been the greatest reward for me as a father. I realize I have two daughters who are their own person with their individual goals and drive. Therefore I could not expect them to obtain their goals in the same manner.

Taylor, my firstborn, is competitive, much like I am. Her main goal is to win, whether it is in sports, grades, or an opinion. School came easy for her, so her mother and I did not have to motivate her. I could not have been prouder when she graduated from college, then later decided she wanted to pursue her doctorate in psychology. She is determined to meet that goal, and I know she will.

Alex, my youngest daughter, does not find college interesting enough to stay the course. She is a go-getter and very stubborn, much like me, but without the competitive spirit. Her main goal is to be independent, above all else. She marches to her own drum, and, as her father, I will not discourage her from moving ahead at her own pace (operative words being 'moving ahead'). As long as she is not going backward in life, I call it 'success.' Alex, while not competitive like her sister, will set goals and obtain them. I remember while she was in high school, I dangled a carrot (a Louis Vuitton purse) and told her if she brought home straight As on her next report card, she could get the purse. She met her end of the bargain, and I had to go shopping. She needed extrinsic motivation, so I had to be prepared to help her along.

Alex and Taylor are two different people with different means of obtaining happiness. I am proud of them and the young ladies they have become. I hold my head up high when I am with them because I wish for all to know that they are my pride and joy.

My wish as a father is to know that my two daughters hold me in high regard as adults, as they did when they were younger. I believe every little girl sees their dad as a hero, but their views may change with maturity. I have tried my best, and I often pray that Alex and Taylor see, learn, and appreciate my efforts. I am far from being perfect and, therefore, have room for improvement. My hope is they did not view my shortcomings as weaknesses but as someone still growing and learning.

I have two posters in my game room that my daughters made as Father's Day gifts on separate occasions. One says, "I'll always be your little girl. You'll always be my HERO." The other says, "A father is someone you look up to no matter how tall you grow." I wish for all fathers to experience the great joy of knowing their children see them as their heroes, even after they are adults. For me, that is one of the ultimate satisfactions of being a father.

I have been married to my high-school sweetheart for 26 years. I have been a father for 24 years and a grandfather for three years. If I were to give advice to a young father, it would be to give constant support to your children's mother. So often, fathers get to be the kids' playmates, but as soon as something goes wrong, it's mommy to the rescue. Fathers are to remember the pressures of a mother go beyond being mothers to the children at home. If she works outside of the home, she is required to give 100% as an employee, 100% as a wife, and most importantly, 100% as a mother. She is the caregiver, the peacemaker, and often the glue that keeps the household together. She is more likely to complain about work-life instead of showing stress from home life, but that does not mean she doesn't need time off from home too. She is a mother 24/7, which includes her days off from work and family vacations. When you, as a young father, want some "time with the boys," remember, she needs some time just for herself, regularly, not just on Mother's Day and Valentine's Day, but regularly. And no, time alone with you is not in her best interest, for when she is with you, just like the children, you need care as well.

Ask her regularly, "Is there anything I can do to make your life easier?" She may be the type never to complain, so watch more than listen for a response. As I previously mentioned, she may not verbally express her needs, but if you are paying attention, you will know without her saying anything. Trust me when I say being able to anticipate her needs will be more appreciated than her having to tell you what she needs.

I would also advise young fathers to be patient with themselves. There is no school that teaches us how to be a father. Life is the teacher on that subject, so lessons learned from your own father, good or bad, should help determine what you will and will not do as a father. Do your very best as a father because, for each of your children, you have one chance. Raise them with love and understanding and the freedom to be themselves. If there is more than one child, treat each as an individual and remember that what works for one may not work for the other. Be creative in how to drive them to succeed and recognize when they need your help in becoming motivated. Remember that you cannot pre-plan their lives for them, for it is theirs to live. They will make mistakes along the way. Just be there when they need help to stand up.

Vincent Alan Rhodes

Vincent Rhodes was born in Cleveland, Ohio, to William and Betty Rhodes. He graduated from John F. Kennedy High School, Northwestern University with a Bachelor of Science in Mechanical Engineering, and General Motors Institute with a Master of Science in Manufacturing Management.

Vincent has been married for 34 years to Michelle Jeffries Rhodes. They have two children, Audrei Jeffries and Alan Rhodes, and twin grandchildren, Peyton and Kelvin Jeffries.

He worked for General Motors for 33+ years in various positions, including product engineer, test engineer, test engineering manager, manufacturing supervisor, maintenance supervisor, aftermarket manager, training manager, and 3rd shift Area Manager.

Currently, Vincent is a building substitute teacher for Sandusky High School, a position he enjoys because it allows him to give back to the children.

He served twelve years as the Sandusky City School's Booster Club president and currently serves as president of the City of Sandusky Civil Service Commission, where he has been an active member for the past 16 years. In addition, Vincent has served on the Board of Trustees of the Sandusky Library for the past 16 years and is a member of the Library's Lange Trust.

Vincent is a member of Kappa Alpha Psi Fraternity Incorporated. He currently resides in Sandusky, Ohio.

Facebook – Vincent Alan Rhodes

Instagram – vincentalanrhodes

Email – varhodesnu@gmail.com

CHAPTER 11

A Father's Path: Lessons, Rewards & Legacy

Vincent Rhodes

Fatherhood is a responsibility to the individuals in your life to nurture, guide, instruct, support, and provide for their livelihood. Fatherhood is one of the most important responsibilities that I have taken on in my life. It is also one of the most gratifying. I was blessed to grow up with my father in my life. My father, William Rhodes, taught me the importance of education, hard work, and keeping a job to bring in income. He worked two jobs most of the time that I lived at home. His primary job was working the swing shift at Lubrizol Corporation. His second job was  as a taxi driver until he began umpiring baseball and softball games. The most important accomplishment of my father's life for me was to be an example or a benchmark of what a father should be. He did not do everything right, but I have been able to decide what type of father I wanted to be based on how he treated our family. I tried to use the good things that he accomplished and discard the bad.

I grew up with my mother, Betty Rhodes, and my father. My father graduated from Central High School, and my mother graduated from John Adams High School, both in Cleveland, Ohio. They met while attending Kent State University. My mom got pregnant at Kent State, and they both dropped out of school and started our family. I have two brothers and two sisters. Dennis Rhodes is the oldest, and if you asked him, he would be happy to tell you that fact. Dennis graduated from John F. Kennedy High School and at his graduation, my father challenged me to be on the stage like my oldest brother. Being on stage meant that you were graduating in the top ten academically in your class. Dennis was ranked No. 10 in his class. Dennis graduated from Northwestern University in Evanston, Illinois. He moved to Detroit and graduated from the University of Detroit Law School. He practiced as an attorney in Michigan and Colorado and is now retired and living with his wife Dona outside of Dallas, in Wylie, Texas. Paul Rhodes is next in the family lineage. Paul is also a graduate of John F. Kennedy High School. Paul went to the Navy after high school and is a retired Licensed Practical Nurse. He is living with and taking care of my mother in Beachwood, Ohio. Diane Harris is my older sister and a John F. Kennedy High School graduate. She graduated from Cleveland State University and is a CPA. She plans to retire this year (2022) from ZF Corporation and enjoy a retired life with her retired husband, Phillip Harris, in Warrensville, Ohio. My younger sister, Michelle Butler, is a graduate of Hawken High School. She graduated from the University of Pennsylvania. Michelle majored in math. She worked for Verizon for over 30 years and retired as one of its top executives. She lives with her retired husband, Nate Butler, in Olney, Maryland.

My father and brothers encouraged me to get my first job, a paper route on 143rd Street. My father and mother helped me on Sundays because the papers were too big and heavy for my shopping cart. I started that job in the seventh grade, and I kept it until I graduated from high school. At my high school graduation, I walked on stage and was ranked No.10 academically out of over 500 students in my class at John F. Kennedy High School in Cleveland, Ohio. I received a full scholarship for my freshman year at Northwestern University, Evanston, IL, where I was enrolled in an engineering co-op program with NASA.

Within a few days of arriving on campus at Northwestern University, an upperclassman named Jo Jo Jasper sought me out on campus. He made sure that we met, and afterward, he showed me around campus and introduced me to a lot of the students on campus. He was a chemical engineering major, so he showed me around the engineering building (Tech) and introduced me to many engineering students. His help was invaluable because it helped me have a smooth transition from high school to the college environment. Most of the other freshman students thought I was an upperclassman because I knew so many people. The university did not provide meals to the students on Sundays, so I went over to my sister-in-law's apartment to eat every Sunday. Flora (Sponge) Rhodes was my oldest brother's first wife, and she fed me well and took good care of me.

I made it a point to go to class every day, and I rewarded myself by going to the gym and playing basketball or any other sport I desired after class. I got involved in playing intramural sports during my first quarter in college. I played on a 3-on-3 basketball team with Gregory Hodge and Kevin Ellis, and we ended up winning the 3-on-3 basketball championship.

In my second quarter on campus, I decided to try to walk on the varsity baseball team. I ended up meeting the baseball coach while the team was playing fall baseball. He told me that fall baseball was almost over and that I could try out in the winter. It was not easy showing what you could do indoors in the frigid winters of Chicago, but I gave it my best shot, and I made the team. I didn't play much during my freshman baseball season, so I ended up pledging Kappa Alpha Psi Fraternity, Inc. in the spring quarter. I pledged with Brian Pharr, Steve Scott, Danny Scotten, and Greg Hodge. We completed our pledge ship and became members of Kappa Alpha Psi Fraternity Inc. Steve is a Northwestern graduate and retired from UPS. He is living in Hawaii with his wife, Pam. Danny is a Northwestern graduate and is the Pastor of Alpha Baptist Church of Willingboro, New Jersey, and lives in Burlington, New Jersey with his wife Linda. Greg is a Northwestern graduate and a practicing attorney. He is currently running for mayor of Oakland, California. Brian left Northwestern before graduating, and we have not heard from him.

I helped to facilitate the crossing of three lines of brothers into the bond of Kappa Alpha Psi Fraternity. I must mention the names of each of these brothers because I did my best to instill good values and qualities into each of them. They are my brothers, and we are still close friends to this day: Gerald Green, John Jones, Rod Archer (sadly passed in January 2010), Wade Griffith, Mike Nixon, John Lane (sadly passed in September 2019 from pancreatic cancer), Mark Caselberry, Yaw Ofosu, Kevin Villars, Dwain Perry, Randy Dixon, Chris Williams, John Ray, Steve Moore, Victor Adams, Mike Sommers, and Alex Booker. We were fortunate to have many talented athletes that joined the fraternity, and we played intramural flag football and 5-on-5 basketball. We went to the championship game two years in a row in flag football, and we won the first year and lost the second year. We went to the championship game in 5-on-5 basketball, and we lost. We also played in a championship game in a Memorial Day 5-on-5 basketball tournament. Our fraternity team played against a team of junior college basketball players that lived in the Chicago area but played all over the country. It was one of the best and most exciting basketball games that I ever played. We played two halves with a 20-minute running clock, and we ended up losing 86-84. My fraternity brothers were much more than athletes. In the group of brothers that I pledged, there are lawyers, a dentist, doctors, ministers of music, actors, coaches, and a computer network analyst. My association with these brothers helped me steer my children because through them I could see the possibilities for my children's lives. These brothers came from all over the United States and Africa. I realized my children could make it from wherever they came from as long as they put in the work. My job was to steer their actions in the right direction.

I graduated from Northwestern University with a degree in mechanical engineering. I started working at General Motors in Sandusky, Ohio, as a College Intern in Training. I met a lady at General Motors named Michelle Jeffries. We became close friends for one year. After that year, we dated for six months, became engaged, and got married one year after our first official date. Michelle is a wonderful person and a great soulmate. We have been married for 34 years. She has written three books, but she made me suffer through authoring this chapter alone, and it has been quite an experience. The same year that we were married, I graduated from General Motors Institute with a master's degree in manufacturing management. Michelle had a five-year-old daughter, Audrei Jeffries, when we married, so I became a newlywed and a new father at the same time. Audrei's father was deceased. When we first started dating, Michelle said that I was dating her and Audrei. I accepted that and tried to make plans for the three of us as much as possible. Looking back, that decision made being a father to Audrei easier. Once I accepted that fact, it was time to move on and develop a relationship with Audrei and my wife. I had to pull from my life experiences along with my experience growing up with my father to help me make wise decisions as I was becoming a young father.

When Audrei was 9 years old, we were blessed to have our son, Alan Rhodes. Michelle and I decided we would focus on three items while raising our children: education, developing skills, and traveling.

Education was a natural choice because Michelle's parents, Freddie and Audrey Jeffries, were both retired educators. I ended up being the one helping our children with their homework after school because Michelle was pursuing her bachelor's and master's degrees, which she eventually obtained from the University of Phoenix. We both went to all parent-teacher conferences and any follow-ups with teachers on issues in the classroom. I went to all the swap days where I would go to school for my children and did their work while they got to stay home. We also made sure they went to school every day and were on time.

We emphasized developing skills beyond the classroom because these activities kept them busy, helped identify their interests and talents, and taught them how to compete. Audrei played the violin, volleyball, softball, and cheerleading. Alan played football, baseball, basketball (until 10th grade), and rollerblade hockey (from age 5 to 18 and was really, really good). He also played the trumpet.

Because Sandusky, Ohio, is a small town, we wanted our children to get more exposure to the world and see things they had never seen before. Travel was the way to accomplish this. The furthest trip, outside of visiting 26 states in the U.S. and Canada, was to Europe (France, Spain, and Italy) with Audrei's high school Spanish class. We also did a lot of traveling in the state of Ohio by visiting relatives and going to sports activities for our children's teams.

Audrei graduated from Sandusky High School and moved to Miami, Florida. She graduated from Johnson and Wales University with a culinary degree. She did an internship at the Winter Olympics in Utah. She went back to college and got her master's degree in human resources. She works at Cedar Point in Sandusky, Ohio, in Human Resources. Alan graduated from Sandusky High School and moved to Norfolk, Virginia. He spent his first year and a half at an HBCU, Norfolk State University. He transferred to Wright State University in Dayton, Ohio, and graduated with a degree in education. He lives in Atlanta, Georgia, and works in the Fulton County School System.

So how do you go from early childhood to high school and college to adulthood? The joy of witnessing a child's evolution in a positive direction has been one of the greatest rewards for me as a father, coach, fraternity member, dean of pledges, and mentor. I coached my daughter in softball from kindergarten through high school. I coached my son in baseball from preschool through high school. My goal in coaching was for the young people to enjoy the sport, learn how to compete, and want to continue playing. I had quite a few young people I coached that ended up playing the sport in high school. I have never had a young person I coached or mentored see me in public and disrespect me, making me feel as though I have done something right in our relationship. The respect that these now grown-up individuals show me is the greatest reward I can ever ask for.

I would advise a young father to embrace being a father, accept the challenge, and be willing to sacrifice some of his wants so that his children can be properly taken care of. You can guide your children into the type of adults you want them to be when you are there for them as they grow up. Of course, your child must cooperate to have the best chance of getting through to them. Children are not robots and won't just do everything you tell them to do, but they hear you even when you think they are not listening. They are watching your character and observing if you are practicing what you preach. Your children can turn their lives around with a lot of patience, prayer, and authenticity in your life. The job of a father never ends, but if you put in the work of raising your children and being there for them as they grow up, then your job becomes easier over the years.

Then you move to the next phase of your life and start over with the grandkids. I have twin grandchildren named Peyton and Kelvin Jeffries. The rules are different for being a grandfather, but sometimes you must step in and help to raise them. Many of the same rules apply to your grandkids, but the main thing is that you are helping your children raise them with the values they want to be instilled in their kids. You must have discussions with your children about the direction that you see your grandkids heading and what adjustments need to be made to their schedule and activities that they are involved in. You also must keep a close eye on the kids they interact with and make sure they are a positive influence in their lives. Whether you are raising a male or a female, a person can come into their lives, and they will forget everything you have taught them. You must resort back to patience and prayer until they snap out of it. Proverbs 22:6 says, "Train up a child in the way he should go: and when he is old, he will not depart from it." You must truly believe that.

I want to be specific regarding sacrifices that may have to be made on your journey of fatherhood. The first possibility could be your career choice. Let me be clear. I believe all fathers should work a legal job. The amount of money you make, the shift you work, the distance from your home to your job, the number of hours you work, and the stress level of your job are a few factors that can affect your availability to be a good father to your children. A father's presence in the home is invaluable. Whenever the father is available in the home, he should reinforce the rules of the home: cleanliness, organization, bedtime hours, diet, use of social media, social media content, choice of friends, who is allowed in the house, exercise, and completing homework assignments on time. Whenever rules are not enforced by both parents, it can become overwhelming, and things will easily fall through the cracks. Be involved with the academic activities of your children. Help decide what school they attend (public or private), and be available to help with homework, check on their progress, and meet with their teachers and the principal. Teachers and principals have a totally different attitude when they talk to a father versus a mother or a grandmother. When the father or grandfather is not present at school events, the school blames all the child's issues on the father not being present in their lives. Attend activities you sign your children up for. Your presence shows that the activity is important and that you expect your children to put forth their best effort while respecting the person in charge. Go to as many Doctor appointments as you can so you are aware of the health status of your children. Diet and exercise decisions can be properly made with this knowledge. Treat your partner with love and respect in front of their children. Argue away from the children because your relationship is the example they will put in their memory banks and may try to duplicate in their later years.

I feel strongly that a father should introduce their kids to their belief system in God. Be a member of a church where your children are comfortable, safe, and growing in the knowledge of God. Be involved in the activities the children take part in at the church. The biblical teachings should be followed up at home by the father to emphasize their importance. These are just a few examples of the sacrifices that I made for my children and my family.

The role of the father changes as your children grow older. You go from being a nurturer, tutor, and taxi to more of a counselor and coach. Eventually, after all the discussions, badgering, and negotiations, the children grow and understand their role in the family structure. The understanding is important because the decisions going forward as the children get older become more expensive and can impact the rest of their lives. The father should take part in the decision if they want to continue to taxi the children around or allow the child access to a vehicle. Now the discussion is about your child working to pay for gas and insurance or for you to pay it. Another major discussion is what the children are going to do after high school. Are they going into the workforce, service, trade school, or college, and who is going to pay for the next step? The discussion must be open and honest because the child may not be clear about what they really want to do. Getting this decision right can save you a lot of money and move your child into adulthood a lot faster. The father must monitor this decision closely and be ready to change course if things are not working out for his child. Once your child makes it to the job and profession of their choice, then you should monitor that it is going well. Your child may change jobs and professions, and you should be there to listen and help guide them through the change.

Once your child is established in the job or career they like, encourage them to give back to whatever community they live in. Every community needs volunteers for a multitude of causes. I started out volunteering at the Boys and Girls Club. I was the Sandusky High School Athletic Booster Club President for 12 years. I interacted with two of the co-authors in this book through the Booster Club. I worked with Coach (T. J.) James when he was the head basketball coach at Sandusky High School. Our Booster Club hosted Orlando Pace when his number was retired at Sandusky High School. I have served on the City of Sandusky Civil Service Committee for the past 16 years, serving as President for the past five years, and continue today. I have also served on the Sandusky Library Board for the past 16 years and continue today. As a member of the Sandusky Library, I am a member of the Lange Trust, a sub-committee that works to bring professional talent to perform. The cost is free to the community. Volunteerism takes time and sacrifice. The best thing you can do is to model fatherhood and service to the community and others in front of your children. They know you better than anyone, and they will remember the life you have lived. When you put in the work and make sound decisions, then you will look back on raising your children and have no regrets. You will be a blessing to them, and they will be a blessing to you.

In conclusion, I leave you with two scriptures that you can use as a guide for being a good father. Ephesians 6:4 (New Living Translation) "Fathers do not provoke your children to anger by the way that you treat them. Rather, bring them up with the discipline and instruction that comes from the Lord." Do you wonder why there are so many angry children walking around this country? It could be because of the way their fathers are treating them, they do not have the proper instruction, or they are not being disciplined in love. Proverbs 3:5-6 "Trust in the Lord with all thine heart and lean not unto thine own understanding. In all thy ways acknowledge him, and he shall direct thy paths." No one has all the right answers about parenting your children but God. Lean on Him, and He will direct your paths for your family. Because when it is all said and done, we want everyone to be saved, including our children.

James E. Keys

James Keys was born and raised in Sandusky, Ohio, to the late Ed Keys and Gloria Garr. James was raised on the south side of Sandusky and attended Sandusky High School, graduating in 1984. Playing football, basketball, and running track, he would win the Vic Malinovsky Award for academic excellence, athletic prowess, leadership, and character. James attended the University of Dayton as a Student-Athlete, where he played football and earned a starting position for three years. James won the Most Improved Player award in 1985. He graduated with a B.S. in Marketing in 1988 and earned his MSA in Operations Management in 2002 from Central Michigan University. James spent over 25 years in Foodservice Operations and the last ten years in consultative, mentorship, and education positions. James resides in Dayton, Ohio, and is married to his wife, Lisa, for 29 years. James has two daughters, Jaciya and Peyton, and three grandchildren, Jazz, Santana, and Jada. He enjoys working with youth and helping them fill their toolbox with resources they will need to grow, live, and learn. James also enjoys biking, working out, golfing, reading, and listening to motivational and inspirational podcasts. His favorite book is "Three Feet from Gold," and his favorite podcast is "Secrets to Success."

Keys2anewu@gmail.com

CHAPTER 12

From Intersections 2 Crossroads

James E. Keys

When I was a child, I talked like a child; I thought like a child; I reasoned like a child. When I became a man, I put the ways of childhood behind me.

~ 1Corinthians 13:11 NIV.

Growing up, I often heard this scripture passage, and as I think back, it is so true as to what should happen as we grow and mature. But as I think further, when did I become a man and put the ways of childhood behind me? What situations did I go through that called for a growth mindset versus a fixed mindset? I made many decisions in my life that have  affected me both positively and negatively, but I learned from those decisions. Life is 10% what happens to you and 90% how you react to it!

Growing up in Sandusky, Ohio, and especially on the Southside, I had some excellent role models, beginning with my father, Ed Keys, and my grandfathers, Mr. Corby Keys and Mr. Robert Collins. Among the community role models were Mr. Bill Churchwell, Mr. Bubba Fuqua, and Pastor Curtis Brown. RIH to these patriarchs. These men had some commonality — commitment, neighborhood kids that looked up to them for direction and support, and their mere presence and character imposed the fear of God in you if you got in trouble. Whatever you did wrong, the word would get home before you did. They all had distinctive management and leadership skills, as I saw firsthand how these men carried themselves, raised their kids, and protected their families. I felt comfortable that I could go to any of them to discuss life. They were the foundation of their family and, in many ways, for the neighborhood.

But I must brag about my Grandfather Keys. I spent many days and nights with my Keys grandparents. Da, as we called him, was an amazing man. The engagement he allowed was like no other. If he was hanging paneling or working on a remodel, he allowed me to help. I learned how to staple ceiling tiles and drive a riding lawnmower from Da. If there were enough extra wood pieces from a job, he would be okay with me making hurdles from the pieces. He allowed basketball games in the garage and driveway if there was no disrespect. If there was disrespect, you may go to church on Sunday. Speaking of respect, that is what we gave and what was deserved by Da.

Both sets of my grandparents lived down the street from each other — one on Camp Street and one on Pierce Street. Between were the Churchwell and Brown families. I would see all of them each day on my walk to and from school. When I think of fatherhood, these patriarchs set the standard which I have relied on regularly to determine if I am properly aligned with my family.

I attended Mills Elementary and Adams Junior High School for seventh grade and Jackson Junior High School for eighth grade before hitting high school. In Junior High, I met a girl, and we quickly became friends before becoming boyfriend and girlfriend. We dated off and on through high school, with many breakups. Friends and family told me to open my eyes as I was blindly in love. But there were situations I was unaware of or failed to accept. I had many discussions with my mom and dad about my goals, future, priorities, boundaries, what-ifs, and whatnot. My parents became parents during their junior year of high school, so I listened to them intently. They gave me enough rope to make decisions, but they often reminded me about making smart choices and not repeating their mistakes. I heard them, but I still took many risks that could have been very costly. Time flew quickly, and before I knew it, my girlfriend and I were both graduating and planning a graduation party together. A few months later, I left Sandusky to attend the University of Dayton, where I played for the Dayton Flyers football program.

When I went away to college, my eyes, ears, and heart were truly opened. Life and priorities had changed, and I was awakened to a new lifestyle. Decisions were mine to make. Going to class or not, studying or not, and going home on the weekend or not were decisions I could now make for myself. But as it's said, with freedom comes responsibility.

The competition was seriously different in college football. I played quarterback and defensive back in high school, and we had only three to five receivers. I was recruited by UD to play receiver, and I was one of 20. All 20 were high school standouts. I played on the scout team but felt I was being underutilized. I believed I was deserving to play in games, like in high school. Football was no longer fun or fulfilling. I wanted to quit the team and school after my freshman year. There I was with an opportunity that few people get. I had not taken full advantage of the opportunity, I was now missing home, and I wanted to throw it all away.

It was a memorable discussion with my father that caused me to dig deep into what I wanted. My dad could not play college-level football. Already a father at graduation, his only choice after high school was to get a job. He wanted so much more for me, so he asked me to give it one more year. With this year, he asked me to focus and work hard in the classroom and weight room. I did just that and had a great second semester and off-season. I looked different, felt stronger, and came into camp sitting as one of the top four receivers. During camp, I went to work. I was faster, stronger, and had gained some weight. I was catching balls, making plays, and blocking like no other. Unfortunately, another receiver broke his ankle during camp, and I was elevated. Yes, I was "Next Man Up." What if I had quit? What if I had given up? What if my dad had not stepped in and shared his story with me? I am beyond thankful that my dad stepped in and challenged me to go deeper, look beyond the moment, and consider what could be. My dad challenged me to look at the big picture, to think and dream bigger!

Lessons of fatherhood continued with my dad. Although my mom and dad divorced during my younger years, I remember my dad always being available to me. Regardless if it was teaching me how to ride a bike, playing sports, helping me with a speech, keeping me sharp, taking me on trips, traveling wherever I was performing, or playing a sport in or out of town, my dad always showed up and supported me.

It was year two of football, and I was doing it. I was the starting flanker, having multiple catch games, a few touchdowns here and there, was player of the game a few times, making key blocks, grading out consistently high, and even keeping my grades up. Around week five, I remember getting a call that no one wants to hear before they are ready– my girlfriend was pregnant. What, how, when, why, where? All those questions came into my mind, and then the discussion that I had with my mom and dad suddenly played in my ear — "Set SMART goals; boundaries protect you; stay focused." What had I done? I continued to play the season, but my play seriously declined. My play should have been getting stronger later in the season, but I was distracted by all that was going on. My focus was off, my game changed, my grades fell, and I needed to talk to someone—not just someone. I needed my dad. We talked often as the season continued. He was at my games at home and on the road. We talked about the responsibilities of being a father and that I would need to make some sacrifices. We talked about the financial, emotional, mental, and social impact that would be placed on my life because of this decision and putting childish ways behind me and stepping up. The season ended, and we were 7-3, but I was worried about my next steps. At the award banquet that season in 1985, I was voted the Most Improved Player out of the 100+ players on the team. But I had some decisions to make, and I consulted with my parents, coaches, friends, and God.

After careful consideration, I made the choice to go home for a semester, attend the local BGSU Firelands campus, and be present for the birth of my child. Coming off an exceptionally good, award-winning season, my coaches were at a loss when I told them I wanted to go home and see my daughter be born and help raise her. As a young man with high hopes of success, many thought my hopes and dreams were over. They felt I would leave school, stop playing football, and stay in Sandusky, Ohio, working in the factory as many had done, including my father. Far too often, people that have kids while in school drop out, get a job and let their hopes and dreams fade away. But my parents and coaches would have no part in that. They encouraged me to remain in school for a semester, train, condition, work, and see the birth of my daughter, but be prepared to return to UD and the team in the fall to continue playing football. Our parents assured us they would help raise my daughter and be as supportive as possible. Talk about pressure! I wondered, what's the right move? Will I let Sandusky get the best of me? Will I let the naysayers push me over the edge? Will I fail in school because of the additional responsibility? Pressure, if not handled properly, can cause you to blow your top.

Returning home was tough. As mom and dad said, the social and emotional impacts were challenging. The first month back in town on a different campus with some of my high school friends, their first comment went something like this, "I thought you....." to "Ok, let's hang out." But after the initial round of questions, it was time to buckle down and get to work studying, lifting, conditioning, and working.

My daughter was born on February 2, 1986, and at that moment, my life changed forever. There she was, this beautiful little bundle of joy that was now depending on me to put her in a position to win in this game called life. Life is not measured by the breaths we take but by the moments that take our breath away. This was one of those moments, welcoming me to fatherhood. We are where we are because of the decisions we have made. Our future will be decided by the decisions we make daily. A single decision may not seem like a big deal at the moment; however, the total of our decisions has a compound effect. But we have the power to change the course of our life and our children's lives.

My days drastically changed. I could no longer just get up and go. I had another responsibility other than myself. Diapers, feeding, entertaining, feeding, diapers, entertaining, rinse and repeat. My girlfriend and I would share schedules, plan, sacrifice, and miss sleep for many nights to care for our baby. This was a different life, but it would be my life over the next six months. It was time to report back to camp at The University of Dayton in early August as I had promised. There were discussions about my girlfriend and daughter coming to Dayton with me; however, that did not work out as we were not on the same page. I had goals, dreams, and aspirations, and the best decision was to keep my commitment even though my responsibilities had changed. I questioned whether I was letting my daughter down. The very thought of it weighed heavily on my mind as I returned to Dayton to fulfill my commitment in the fall of 1986.

Playing UD football required me to be locked into the program and avoid as many distractions as possible. During the next four months, I would only see my daughter when she was brought to Dayton for visits. Her mother brought her to Dayton as often as she could, and it was hard to see them leave. I found it very difficult to perform the duties that a father, as I understood it, should be doing. I felt there was a missing link in this experience as a father. The link that a father and child need to create a bond that will last forever. Over the next two years, I would return to my home in Sandusky during the summer, work for ten weeks, and head back to Dayton for school. The relationship with my daughter's mother deteriorated, adding the stress of relationship issues to an already full plate, but I pressed on. By my senior year, my daughter's mother and I had broken up, but I had supportive relationships with my roommates and friends at the University of Dayton. I would experience the extent of these friendships when they stepped up in a major way during the period my daughter lived with me in Dayton. While I had class or practice, the tribe made sure my daughter was cared for. It was a blessing that we still talk about today.

Upon graduation, I remained in Dayton, and weekends and summers were the times that allowed me to be the best father I could be. I missed several "firsts" with my daughter - first steps, first words, and first days of school. I missed the father-daughter dances and first dates. I missed the times my daughter fell, cried, and called my name because I was not there to comfort her. The times I would meet her mother or my parents on State Route 6 to pick up my daughter was the best. However, the drop-off and ride back home without her were the worst. My daughter would cry her little eyes out as we had to nearly force her to go back with her mom or my parents. I will never forget that pain. I would later learn just how much I had missed in experiences with my first daughter, as I had a totally different experience with my second daughter.

In 1989, when my daughter was three years old, I met an amazing young lady. During our first conversations, I shared that I had a three-year-old daughter. This young lady was an encourager, and she accepted my daughter right away. Prior to meeting her, missing my daughter and not in a meaningful relationship, I requested and was granted a job transfer to Cleveland, Ohio. Now closer to my daughter, I could be the father I should be. Having met this amazing young lady and now challenged with a long-distance relationship, I faced a new dilemma. Will this work? Well, it was going so well that I changed jobs and moved back to Dayton. Yes, another time I faced a tough decision that would cause me to leave my daughter. Was I in a better place? Could my daughter move with me? Would my new girlfriend move to Sandusky? All questions that I would need to discuss to determine my next steps and what was best for me. The no's outweighed the yes,' so back to Dayton I went. Over the next few years, weekends and summers were times I would spend with my daughter; however, it became even more challenging than in previous years because of the soured relationship with my daughter's mother. My girlfriend would become my wife four years later, in 1993. We married, but sadly, without my daughter's presence. Pressure. What's the right move? Why did my daughter's mother not allow her to be in the wedding? Do I make a big deal of it or let it ride? Pressure, if not handled properly, will cause you to blow your top.

My wife and I would have a baby girl a year into our marriage. This baby girl is our miracle child as we had an unfortunate situation happen before and after her birth. It was while raising my second daughter I realized what fatherhood is all about. I understood even better that the men I looked up to as a child had it absolutely right. There were experiences I witnessed with my second daughter because of my presence. Things I missed with my first daughter I could now take part in with my second daughter. I witnessed the "firsts" - first words, first steps, riding a bike, falling off the bike, coaching sports teams, attending parent-teacher conferences, and attending Dad and Donuts. This time I was present, and I was in a much better position to make these things happen. When we could, we would be sure to include both daughters as much as possible for events, concerts, family gatherings, and more. However, sometimes the weekend parental transfer was a challenge and, sometimes, did not happen. Sometimes my older daughter did not want to come, and it hurt, leaving me to ask, "Why? What did I do? What was said or done?" Well, I know what I did, and it was that I left my daughter with her mom. I left her without her father to provide the fatherly parenting, love, and support that she deserved. I left her not understanding what it was to set proper boundaries, as my parents had taught me. I left her to figure things out when she was home alone. I left her alone. When I look at the early years of both of my daughters, I realize there were moments I had with one that I did not have with the other, and I can't get those opportunities back, but I can do all that I can to make it up. That is what I did, as much as I could.

It was this fatherly void that led to my daughter getting pregnant and having her first child at age 16. I was devastated as I let my daughter down. Many questions go through my head as to what if I had lived in Sandusky and could have been more present with my daughter. What if I had been more assertive in my desire to have my daughter live with me? What if I had the financial means to fight for my daughter? What if, what if, what if? These questions remain, and the message of "never quit" that my father instilled in me came back to the surface. The "never quit" mentality now challenges me to be present with my grandsons and granddaughter.

Today, I can say that I am immensely proud of my daughters. Even though my oldest was put into a position where she should not have been at a young age, she has prospered. Even though my youngest had both parents throughout her upbringing, there were still things she went through with both parents working that she should not have, but she has prospered. As a dad, I often wondered if I did it right. I was not perfect; I was far from it, but I also know there is no perfect father other than the Almighty Father. But I can say with a resounding yes, I am OK with the decisions and choices I made as they were learning lessons, and my daughters have been open to listening and learning from those decisions.

The decisions we make as young men play a role not only in our lives but in the lives of those we touch every day, including our future spouse, kids, grandkids, parents, teammates, and many whom we have not even met yet. Things have not always been easy, as we all go through tough and challenging times. However, we have prospered. We wanted different, which was, many times, better. My girls are both working professionally, have purchased homes, and have taken control of their lives. One has kids, and the other is focused on her career. I genuinely believe that my older daughter taught my younger a lesson not necessarily through words but through actions. My girls are different, no doubt; however, they were raised differently. Different is okay in some situations, as you can learn from one another. What works for one may not work for the other.

As a father, I have learned to be open to listening, providing my thoughts, and advising. If they choose to listen or not, they will make decisions that will ultimately impact their lives, either positively or negatively, depending on the decision. We are where we are today because of the decisions we made every day. As fathers, we are the thermostat. We initiate action to change the temperature of the environment that we are in. There are times we must cool things down by being assertive and identifying the problem to take appropriate action for a positive outcome. Then sometimes, we must increase the temperature to address things that are not going as planned—again, with an assertive approach to get into the right position. This is where the pressures of fatherhood come to life. I'm often questioning, "Am I doing the right thing? Did I show them the right way?" If not handled correctly, pressure will cause you to blow your top and possibly do something you may regret later.

The decisions we make from ages 15 to 30 will be some of the most critical decisions we will ever make. The outcome of some decisions may be with you for the rest of your life. Think I'm kidding—ask someone or look at my story. I can share that my decisions in my teenage years, the twenties, and thirties are having a drastic impact on my life today, some good and some opportunities.

Over the years, I have learned many valuable lessons as a father, but I've learned the importance of being present for your family, working on yourself, writing your goals, never quitting, whatever you are doing, keep showing up, surrounding yourself with positivity, changing the input if you don't like the output, and not allowing obstacles to impede achieving your hopes and dreams. They may be delayed but not denied.

Throughout life, you will have many Intersections. "Our ability to make a difference in not only our life but the lives of others must be partnered with commitment and determination of goodwill, but most importantly, GOD Will. Living good is not the same as living Godly."–Bro. Pastor Kris Petersen.

Turn those Intersections into Crossroads!

Alexander Pezo

Alexander Pezo is a notable *fashion designer, image consultant*, and *author*. He is also a *devoted coach, mentor*, and *friend*. His business savvy and a love for design and people, make him the perfect branding and style connoisseur. His continued passion for guiding individuals to "Bet on themselves" has served as an inspiration to many.

However, expanding the brand beyond fashion has been the target of Alexander Pezo. He has written his second and third books, "Polish Your Appearance A Gentleman's Guide to Style and Image" in addition to "Polish Your Appearance a 30-Day Devotional." He is also Disc certified and Wilson Learner trained

With that to his acclaim, Alexander Pezo has been featured on BETHER, My People Podcast featuring the Welthe Guy, Candid Conversation featuring Stacy Bryant, The Stoney Love Show, TAT Ministry "Featuring" Tia Tat Talley the Atlanta Voices 100 Yards of Sports featuring Vincent Turner, WCEG Network the Wood, 106RadioLive.com, Gwen's Business Corner, & DPRGRADIO.COM featuring Terrence Andre.

Alexander received a Proclamation from the City of Atlanta for his work in the community and contribution in fashion. Alexander was featured in the February 2020 Voyage ATL, December 2019 cover of Black Business of Atlanta, May 2019 cover of ASPE Magazine, March 2018 cover of Bonheur Magazine, featured in Sheen Magazine September 2016, and Young Black Entrepreneurs 2016. The brand's designs have graced the runways at Georgia Peach Fashion Week May 2016 and Plitz New York Fashion Week September 2016. Alexander also served as The Commercial Wardrobe Consultant for one season of the Christian View (2017). In 2020 Alexander made his directorial debut in "The Trek" which is a journey about his life.

Alexander stays humble and hungry as he continues to build his brand and venture into the private sector with its inaugural Polish Your Appearance Black Tie Scholarship Gala. He often says, "I have never seen a U-Haul behind a funeral procession. We cannot take the knowledge and resources with us." Alexander's forward-thinking mentality stems from his 28 years of Senior Leadership and Staffing industry experience, (currently) as the Market Director for Northeast Atlanta for a top two firm in the world.

Pezo and his wife Yolanda just launched their first Airbnb in Atlanta that is also featured on Peerspace and Giggster. The name of the company is Denam Luxury Spaces.

Alexander is the father to three amazing kids, Bria Kathleen, Milana Alexis and Jaxon Alexander as well as a supportive husband and best friend to Yolanda Denise. He and his family reside in Gwinnett County in the Grayson School District. In addition, Pezo has a master's degree in athletic administration from Ohio University and Bachelor of Arts in English-Journalism from Tennessee Tech.

SOCIAL MEDIA & LINKS | IG: @alexanderpezobrand| FB: Alexander Pezo Brand |Twitter Alexander Pezo_| LinkedIn: https://www.linkedin.com/in/alexander-pezo-745693190/

CHAPTER 13

Redemptive King

A Fatherless Trek to Fatherhood

Alexander Pezo

"There is nothing functional in generational dysfunction.*"* No, really, there isn't. William Earl Bennie Fred Mays was my grandfather. A 6'2" nearly 300-pound imposing figure that drove tractor-trailer trucks for Wilson Freight in the '70s and early '80s. He was the husband to Magnolia Mays, father to daughters Deborah Jean, Yvonne (my mother), Sandra Denise, fraternal twins Marlene and Darlene, and youngest William Earl Mays. They say, "Men love their daughters and raise their sons."  However, how can you love your daughters if you mistreat their mothers? Likewise, how can you raise your son to become anything other than what he's witnessed daily?

All I could think about at age 24 when Bria Kathleen, my firstborn, arrived were the many days of dysfunction I had lived through. How in the hell would I learn to be a father on the fly knowing I had two prior generations of *"horrible.com"* fatherless examples? From all recollection, my grandfather loved to *"tie one on,"* as they say. He enjoyed the nightlife and fraternizing. Thinking back, my grandfather, as the story goes, was escorted out of the house by my mother and Aunt Deborah Jean in, let's just say, an "aggressive manner." He never returned to the house again. I would be remiss if I didn't say thank you for loaning me the $3,500 down payment to assist with the purchase of my first home. Looking back on what I was exposed to set the stage for me wanting to avoid a "Fatherless Trek to Fatherhood." However, this was my start to being able to see a different end game for myself.

At a very young age, multiple opportunities presented themselves for me to become a statistic or "product of my environment." However, my mother, Yvonne Alexandria Mays, nicknamed "Red" for the color of her hair, as mentioned in my previous book *"Polishing Your Appearance,"* started to shape and mold me into what she hoped would one day come to fruition.

After attending public school for three years, Red boldly decided to bus me 45 minutes from the Northside of Cincinnati to the Eastside to attend Saint Francis de Sales for 3rd and 4th grade. In her attempt to find the best academic fit for me, I went on to St. Mark for the 5th grade and eventually finished middle school, 6th to 8th grade, at St. Cecilia's. This was a predominantly Caucasian school in the middle-class neighborhood of Oakley. However, St. Francis de Sales ultimately exposed me to kids from various cultures other than just Black.

Red placed me in this environment because, as she would say, "Everyone wants to grow, but growth is uncomfortable." In other words, she knew I would get ridiculed by some students at the school. She also knew this would force me to either "Polish My Appearance" or level up in the areas I severely needed to or receive constant teasing.

To make things more challenging, I had to switch teams in baseball, which led me to play baseball for one of the most prominent and generationally wealthy families of Cincinnati in the Sweeneys. This team comprised a hodgepodge of kids from all over the school district.

This team comprised players from stable, middle-class two-parent households, primarily. Being exposed to this environment broadened my horizons and forced me to learn how to communicate differently. The three years that my mom invested in my Catholic School education ultimately changed my environment and made the transition seamless.

Looking back, Red was attempting to teach me "priority-based education," how to become well-rounded, as well as "how the other half lived." More importantly, she told me that priority-based education meant that she was sacrificing for my education now, hoping I would not have to pay for it later. This strategy is commonly used in more affluent and suburban communities that use quality-free or private, or catholic education to put their kids in advantageous positions for their futures. Somehow my mom was able to make ends meet and put me through Catholic school from the 3rd through 8th grade.

The investment that my mom made in me, though tough at times, started the process of me being able to overcome any thoughts of a "Fatherless Trek to Fatherhood." The most impressive part of this process was that she made it happen as a single parent. That said, the impact of Red's decisions on my life was paramount. Her guidance and direction were ahead of the curve at such a young age. In fact, for my freshman year, she sent me to one of the premier schools in Ohio, the Summit Country Day School. To this date, The Summit Country Day School is second to none when it comes to producing students with high character, integrity, and the moral fiber to excel higher in academia and life. Knowing what my mom had been through in her life explains why she made these decisions for me, that I could later manifest positively (just wait and see).

After Robert Alexander, my dad (16) and my mother (15) gave birth to me on February 6th, they then had my sister Natasha 11 months later on January 16th. However, she and I would not "officially" meet until 49 years later. Let that sink in for a minute. Six degrees of separation is the idea that all people are six or fewer social connections away from each other. In this case, my sister, whom I had never met because of being put up for adoption, attended Walnut Hills High School, which is .3 miles away from the home where my mother and I lived. She then went to school with my childhood friend Karl Brown. If that was not close enough, I dated one of her best friends, Kiva, who lived in the same community as Natasha and my father. My mom went to her grave and never revealed the real story behind what happened with my sister. However, as the story would have it, my mom told me she was sexually assaulted as a teenager and became pregnant. In her words, she was "Pro-life" and decided to put Natasha up for adoption. So, the morning Natasha reached out to our oldest daughter, Bria Kathleen, because her Ancestry search revealed that her mother, Yvonne Alexandria, was her grandmother, she knew there was an obvious connection (me). I, in turn, reached out to our father to see if he would share any additional details and he stated, "Your grandmother Mag told me to go home because the baby was stillborn, and Red would contact me." This web of lies was all created because of the compound of bad decisions with even more questionable ones. The trajectory of lives was ultimately altered for years to keep an appearance that was not real. Babies making babies made bad decisions only to have those in charge of their lives at the time making choices that left others without answers and possibly scarred for life.

If this is not ironic enough, my wife Yolanda attended the same high school as my sister. This is also the same school that renowned Director Stephen Spielberg attended. One may say, why mention Spielberg? Because this feels like a movie script to me (Lol). My father, from all indications, spiraled out of control as a teenager, and his parents felt that my mother was not good enough for him. This led to him enlisting in the Army without warning to my mother.

This left my mother at 17 years of age with one child under two years old and another that had recently been adopted. I truly feel this speaks to my mom being broken and potentially feeling alone, as if she was the black sheep of the family early on. She dated a gentleman named Greg in high school and into her 30s, but they never married. They lived together for over a decade. He was a nice guy, but my mother struggled to find herself during the relationship. Greg went on and had an affair with another woman. During his affair, the woman became pregnant and conceived a child that my mom knew nothing about initially. Greg ultimately married the woman. My mom was left alone to figure it out and pick up the pieces for the second time in a row. Two generations and the first three examples of men I encountered - my grandfather, father, and Greg - came short of being an example of fatherhood. Remember this adults, as we make decisions we feel only affect us, kids don't get a chance to choose their parents. Knowing this, I consciously sought and spoke into existence what was meant for my life. At 15, while in the Purcell-Marian High School cafeteria, I met a man that would change my life forever. My history teacher Fred Geraci became a mentor, trusted advisor, and friend for nearly 40 years of my life thus far. He taught me things that most young men, more importantly, Black men, will never learn. He got me summer jobs working on tennis courts, showed me how to be accountable, supported me through trials and tribulations, and never wavered. Allowing me to be around him and his family provided me the opportunity to visualize how this could one day be my "new normal."

The lessons he taught me and my experiences growing up in Cincinnati, Ohio prepared me for life after athletics. I had just finished my collegiate basketball career and taken my first sales and finance job in the auto industry eight days before becoming a father. As a 24-year-old father, I knew it would be a process. I wasn't married to Bria's mother, lived in a different state, and was still finding myself. No matter the circumstances, I had to break the generational curses from "A Fatherless Trek to Fatherhood." I had to become a "Redemptive King," if you will. I vowed to remember the mistakes of the men that had come before me in my life. I had to become a blessing and not a burden to Bria.

But the initial trek was just the opposite. Overcoming multiple generations of dysfunctional fatherhood, was a challenge. The closest family example I had to be age-wise was my uncle. He and I were six years apart. He was the baby of my mom's siblings and had been incarcerated for 11 years at this point. I was more of an example for him as opposed to him for me. I was teaching myself how to avoid becoming another statistic, and parent all at the same time, which would be no small order.

As my journey started, I began traveling five hours one way every other week to North Carolina to see Bria. I was granted a four-hour visitation. At this point, I had just been promoted to Finance and Insurance Manager. With that came long hours every Monday to Saturday and only having Sundays off. I would leave at 5:30 a.m. (EST) to arrive in Western North Carolina on time. I can admit, at times, I was late, which caused my ex to cancel my visitation. Looking back, I do not blame her, but emotions affected the circumstances at the time. The only thing that I come back to is - "Kids don't get a chance to choose their parents." I had to figure out how to navigate the terrain of fatherhood, whether it was planned or not. At this time in life, my experiences taught me, "Tough times don't last, but tough people do." As the legendary basketball coach Bobby Knight would say, "Mental to physical is as 4 is to 1." The ups, downs, and growing pains over the next 14 years and the many trips from Tennessee to North Carolina and then Cincinnati to Tennessee allowed me to build a bond between myself and Bria that will never be broken.

After years of holiday and summer break visits, at 15, Bria started living with my first wife and myself full-time. As a former collegiate athlete, my promise to her mother was that we would not have to pay for college if she came to live with us in Cincinnati. Bria attended my alma mater Purcell-Marian and ironically had the pleasure of being taught by my mentor Fred Geraci. Besides being around great people, after her sophomore year in high school, she and I decided that it made sense for her to focus on academics and volleyball and retire from the game of basketball (Lol). This turned out to be the best decision for the immediate future.

At the time, I was working as a Sports Market Manager in the hotel industry. I would spend my lunch breaks sending emails, letters, and videos to college coaches. The decision that we made to have her stop playing basketball and focus on volleyball was paying dividends. Bria had gone from starting varsity as a sophomore and finishing 3rd in the city in blocks to one of the best players in the city. She finished 11th in her class academically, was 1st team all-city, 2nd team all-district, and was offered a full-ride volleyball scholarship to Northern Michigan University. Focusing on Priority Based Investing, which means pay now to avoid paying later, paid off. This was a huge accomplishment, considering Bria had only played the game for four full years. In addition, her college recruitment process allowed me to spend a great deal of quality time with her. Remember, "You can make more money, but you can't make more time." My three male examples of what not to do as a parent and the mentorship of Fred Geraci and countless others were manifesting positively. The "Fatherless Trek to Fatherhood" that I had over the years was paying off years later through Bria.

Sent: Mon Apr 09 16:27:03 CDT 2012
To: briamays3@gmail.com

Dear Bria,

I am pleased to inform you that an athletic scholarship to Northern Michigan University is being offered to you for the 2012-13 academic year. Please thoroughly read the attached document and feel free to contact me with any questions.

Per NCAA rules we are also obliged to share information about organized competition as it relates to the NCAA. For more information on organized competition **click here.**

To accept the athletic scholarship under the conditions specified in the Tender of Financial Assistance and the National Letter of Intent, please print and sign both documents. For your personal records you are to keep one copy of the NLI and one copy of the Tender of Financial Assistance. Return one signed copy of the NLI and one signed copy of the Tender of Financial Assistance to: ….

Seeing the words, 'we are pleased to inform you that an athletic scholarship to Northern Michigan University is being offered to you for the 2012-13 academic year,' was a proud father moment. The phrase "I want to leave a legacy" is often said in the black community. However, you must plan the work and work the plan. To me, the word legacy means putting your family in a situation that is a blessing and not a burden. Teaching your kids the value of priority-based education, which means you pay now to avoid paying later, is key. Bria attending Purcell-Marian High School, more notably the same school that NFL Hall of Famer Roger Staubach, NBA Champion Derrick Dickey, NFL former player and current Official Terry Killens, and Men's USA Volleyball Olympian Max was worth the sacrifice. To be in the financial position that allowed me to put Bria in a school with such history academically and athletically was a great feeling. Hence, paying now meant college should be free with minimal financial obligation later. To leave a legacy for my kids, it was imperative that Bria not be plagued with the financial burden most have after five and a half years of college. This is the average timeframe it takes to finish a four-year undergraduate degree. After her first year at NMU, her scholarship was reduced to 50% instead of full.

In this situation, I have seen parents leave their kids at the school to save embarrassment, not thinking of the long-term ramifications this will cause them financially. I decided to place Bria in a Junior College, Grand Rapids Community College. After one year at GRCC, Bria graduated and moved in with my second and current wife, Yolanda, and me. At the time, she did not have a scholarship offer, but as God would have it, a coach from Augusta University was watching film on another player and discovered Bria. She offered Bria a scholarship under the pretense that the first semester would not be paid. Yolanda, I, and Bria's mom split the cost. This meant, yet again, no college tuition for Bria. She played parts of two seasons at Augusta before earning her degree in Psychology. However, the legacy aspect of the story is that she graduated with less than $2,000 in debt. Essentially, Bria went to school free. Yolanda, I, and Bria's mom ensured that she had a $150,000 head start in life. Now that is a legacy move. Instead of the funds Bria would have been bogged down with paying back student loans, she could now put toward purchasing her first home. Bria now lives in Dacula, Georgia, with her husband Bo and daughter Sarai (2 years old).

The legacy continues as a year before Bria came to live with us in Cincinnati, her sister Milana Alexis was born. I still remember watching the classic two OT 74-72 game between Ohio State and Sienna Men's Basketball game late on March 20, the day before Milana's birth. Now, just like that, she is 13 years old and one of the best volleyball players in the Midwest. Last summer her team with the Munciana Volleyball Club finished 3rd at the Nationals in Orlando, and she made the All-American Team. More importantly, she is a straight-A student in the Hamilton Southeastern School District. Milana has been an excellent example for her 5-year-old brother Jaxon. She is the middle sibling to Bria and Jaxon, from my first marriage. As I stated at the beginning of the chapter, "Kids Don't Get to Choose Their Parents." My learning to become a better father, husband, and person has never clouded my perspective on how to be the best dad for each of my kids, which has led me to become "A Redemptive King." A Redemptive King is a male ruler of an independent state of mind acting to save someone from error or evil: I refer to this as "the healing power of redemptive love." Through my "Fatherless Trek to Fatherhood," I learned everything I needed to know about becoming a less-than-stellar dad. In fact, I had the recipe memorized on just how to repeat the cycle three times over. However, my zest to become a better version of myself from Bria Kathleen to Milana Alexis and now Jaxon Alexander will continue to pay dividends for our family's legacy.

They say that "Men love their daughters and raise their sons." When it comes to Jaxon, I am doing everything it takes to ensure he can accomplish everything the first time that it took me to become three times over. Now five, Jaxon is well adjusted academically, reading on a 3rd-grade level, extremely likable, and has a heart of gold. While each of our kids exudes a piece of our future, Jaxon carries the mantle and is provided the opportunity to be his best self through the lessons that Yolanda and I continually teach him. I am a believer that when you make a conscious decision to live righteously, you can self-correct and redirect the ways of your past through the eyes of your future (Bria Kathleen, Milana Alexis, and Jaxon Alexander).

Without Yolanda, there would be no Alexander Pezo. She pushes me in every possible way to become a better person than I was the day before. She has helped me to realize that "Individual success is only one-third of what you can accomplish with the right life partner." I learned to be a true *Redemptive King,* I needed a stable, supportive Queen. In Yolanda Denise, I found that. Thank you for all the love, laughter, friendship, and peace you bring to life and our home. This has taught me how to lead our home and kids as partners. Your willingness to share your love and heart to make room for Natasha and me to grow our bond as brother and sister, as well as "Swedish Twins," is unmatched!

To those coming to the end of reading this chapter, please take note that this is only the beginning of chapters that will be written about my sister Natasha and me. Our story promises to be an inspiration to the many individuals with siblings that have been through similar situations. That stated, "Tasha," I can tell you that our mother, Yvonne Alexandria, is smiling down as you finish your Doctorate. Who would have ever thought that a teenage mother would produce such successful siblings from a parental, academic, community, corporate, and philanthropic perspective?

If this is not redemption, then I do not want to be redeemed! Stay tuned for the next chapter and remember:

A Redemptive King is a male ruler of an independent state of mind acting to save someone from error or evil: I refer to this as "the healing power of redemptive love" through My "Fatherless Trek to Fatherhood,"

Abdur Karim

Abdur Karim is a native Detroiter who graduated from Michigan State University. Go Green!! Abdur has worked in the consulting and workforce planning industry for over 22 years. He enjoys fitness, playing golf, and traveling with his family when he is not working. Abdur is a die-hard Spartans, Lions, Pistons, and Tigers fan. Abdur currently lives in the metro Atlanta area with his wife of 20 years, Qiana, and their two sons, Jordan and Jaylen. Abdur helped to start a Little League organization in metro Detroit for football and cheer serving over 200 youth yearly. Abdur is the son of Wali Karim and Kamilah Karim-Tipton and is the youngest of four. Fatherhood to Abdur is an honor. His greatest accomplishment is being a father to his sons and a father figure to all the kids he coached.

Abdur Karim

karimabdur@yahoo.com

twitter: abdurkarim313

Instagram: kikindooley

CHAPTER 14

Quality Time

Abdur Karim

Being a father is one of the greatest gifts a man can receive in a lifetime. But for a first-time father, it's also one of the scariest times in life. When I became a father, I was so worried that I would do or say something wrong. I learned quickly that we do and say so many things wrong that you just accept it as part of a father's trial-and-error process and learn from your mistakes.

As I began thinking about my path as a father, I couldn't help but reflect on my parents and my childhood.

My father and mother were born and raised in Lagrange, Georgia, about 45 minutes southwest of Atlanta. My mom and dad grew up within a mile of each other, and they, along with my aunts and uncles, went to the same high school. My parents moved to Detroit, Michigan after marriage, and while my mom finished school, the entrepreneurial spirit that was passed down from my grandfather to my father had begun.

My father started a few companies over time, while my mother graduated with her degree in education. My father worked long hours, and we all understood he was doing what he thought was best to take care of our family. My mother, like many mothers, was the rock that kept all of us moving in the right direction.

My father had a company that delivered lost luggage, and he worked many long days. It was the best thing ever whenever I rode along with him because I was able to spend time with him while also seeing different areas of the city. As a kid, both were so cool to me. The one-on-one quality time I was able to spend with my father is what I remember and cherish most.

There are some memories as a kid you never forget, and they mean the world to you. Like the trips we took as a family, long drives to Lagrange and to North Carolina, stopping at the mall, and even the Econo Lodge hotel in Kentucky, where we stayed on one of our trips to Georgia.

I am the youngest of four. I have two older brothers and an older sister. As the youngest, I watched closely how my older siblings were being treated, and I noticed some differences. I always said, "When I grow up, I'm going to treat all my kids the same." That was always my goal until I had kids and I saw how different they are from one another. All of a sudden I got it, and I thought, man, I'm glad my parents showed me that!

Being raised on the west side of Detroit on Murray Hill, we did not have everything we wanted, but we had what we needed. I knew my parents worked hard to make sure we had our needs and tried their best to give us what we wanted. But yes, sometimes I was a brat and complained when I didn't get my way.

When our neighborhood began to change, I vividly remember my parents focusing on getting us moved to a better neighborhood. They sealed into my memory that a parent's job is to protect the family, and they were persistent until a new neighborhood became our reality. While I didn't understand much about being an entrepreneur at the time, I later recognized that ups and downs are part of the business. I was so young that I could not tell when we were going through tough times, but I am sure my older brothers and sister knew what was going on. I did recognize, however, when my father's health began to affect his ability to work. But he kept grinding for his family despite his declining health. In the meantime, my mom was the constant rock for the entire family, which kept us moving forward.

Going to high school can always be an adjustment for kids. I played football and basketball and ran track, keeping busy throughout the school year and summer with sports. High school was not hard for me, as I was able to keep my grades above a 3.0 GPA. Playing sports kept me away from a lot of the trouble that some of my friends ran into. It's amazing when you have kids in different activities how they avoid many of the obstacles and challenges some kids go through. That's why it's so important to invest in the youth and our communities. Many coaches in our neighborhoods were father figures to a lot of kids. They were the reason some kids made it.

I was blessed to have both parents in the same household to make sure I was going down the right path, and if I was not heading in the right direction, they were able to re-direct me. I also had great coaches that kept us straight. I was blessed to be part of the winning 4x100 state championship relay team during my senior year of high school, which was so exciting; I will never forget that day. I also remember my dad could not make it. I know I will not be present for all of my children's highs and lows, but I vowed to myself that I would do everything in my power to be there as much as possible.

After high school, I was blessed to be accepted to Michigan State University and follow in my big sister's footsteps. I was also blessed to run track during my first couple of years at Michigan State. Earlier I mentioned how easy high school was for me, but what I did not know was how unprepared I was for college. For the first couple of years, I was barely eligible to run. College was tough because I did not prepare myself for the level of commitment needed to succeed. If I had not been part of the track program, I would not have made it. But my advisor stuck with me and encouraged me every day. Those first two years were a perfect example of not having the fundamental skills and discipline, and how so many young people of color struggle because of a lack of preparation once they arrive on campus.

I still remember the one and only summer I went home. I was able to stay with my oldest brother Yusuf for the summer, which I thought was the coolest thing ever. The conversations I had with my father and my brother Hassan will stick with me forever. My father looked at my grades and said, "This is your life, and you must live with the decisions that you make." He spoke in a very calm voice. I felt like he was saying we have given you everything you need to be successful. Now it's up to you if you choose to use it. My brother Hassan, if you know him, is a little more direct and told me not to come home anymore until I graduate because there was nothing there. That was the PG version of what he said. I look up to my brothers a lot. They have the entrepreneurial spirit of our father and grandfather. Both have started businesses and are doing well for themselves and their families. My sister Rashidah, whom I look up to also, is a graduate of Michigan State University and a successful educator in Georgia. She did not have much to say except, "It's on you." I was able to get back on track with my school courses, and it was my sole focus that made a huge difference.

Back in my college days, you had to pay for long-distance calls, and my part-time job allowed me to make those calls. I always made the effort to call home and talk to my dad more often than usual. I never thought I would ever get this call. I spoke to my dad on the morning of November 24, 1997, and my mom called that evening and asked me to give the phone to my roommate. His expression told it all. My father passed away from a massive heart attack at 49 years old. They drove me home that night, and I could not tell you anything about the ride. I was in shock after hearing that my father had passed away.

I appreciate the quality time I spent with my dad, but I still look at all the times he missed. It is so important to spend as much quality time as possible with your loved ones while you have the chance. Do it today. Tomorrow is not guaranteed.

After the funeral, my mom was doing what she had done our entire life, and that was to keep the family together and keep us moving in the right direction. She told me to go back to school and finish because that is what my father would have wanted me to do.

After my father passed away, I returned to school and graduated. During my last couple of years at Michigan State, I met my wife, and I feel my dad had a part in that. My wife, Qiana, was the best thing that happened to me. Qiana motivated me and encouraged me to pursue my dreams and believe in myself daily. Her encouragement motivated me every day that I stepped into the office to strive for excellence.

My wife Qiana and I were young when we had our oldest son Jordan, who recently graduated from high school and will attend college in the fall. As a first-time father, you begin to worry about things like checking on your newborn to make sure they are breathing. How fast is the car driving behind you? Are these clothes going to irritate their skin? What's the right milk and food? But the biggest thing that keeps me up is making sure I can provide for my kids like my parents provided for us. As a father, you always want to be sure you can provide for your family financially, and if you can't, what impact will that have on the family? This was my motivation every day - to be at work while my wife took care of our son. Society has always told men to work and take care of their families financially, and that is what I intended to do.

As my career began to grow, I started working longer hours. I noticed my son was growing so fast, and I was there but not present. I am blessed to have a wonderful wife that was amazing at managing her career and making sure our boys had everything. As a parent, we always want to provide our kids with everything we had and more. Many times, we focus on materialistic things and miss the importance of spending time with our kids and family. What may seem minor at the time, such as playing with the kids in the yard, putting them on the bus, and attending their school activities, gives our kids a sense of love, security, and significance. And they look for both parents to be present. When Jordan was younger, many times, I would arrive at events late or miss them altogether because of my work schedule, but in the back of my mind, I wanted my five-year-old to understand that Daddy must work so he could have nice things. But I knew the truth: kids want quality time with their parents. They want to look in the crowd and see you there. I noticed Jordan would look in the crowd, make eye contact, and smile when he saw me. It just made me feel so good. My youngest, Jaylen, wanted to know who was going to be at the game before the game even started. Jaylen did not like me traveling at all. Anytime I travel, it's a rough first night for my wife. But like my mom, Qiana is that rock that keeps the family moving in the right direction. Jaylen still does not like me traveling and always wants to know my travel itinerary. As he got older, he always wanted to know if I would be traveling, how long I would be gone, and if I would miss his game. Quality time with their father is what my sons wanted and needed.

I knew any attempts to make Jordan's activities would mean leaving work on time and negatively impact my career. It was not looked upon favorably for fathers to leave on time. I even had one of my directors ask me, "Why can't your wife do it?" He said I need to be at work so people could see that I was dedicated to my career. But I knew the impact my presence and quality time would have on my boys, which was bigger than anybody or anything in the world. I had the reminder of my father passing away from a massive heart attack at forty-nine to help keep my priorities with my family in their proper place.

As a present and active father with your kids, you learn so much about them, but most important is what you learn about yourself. My kids taught me how to be patient and enjoy the moment. My wife and I set a goal to create experiences for our kids. I could not tell you what gifts I received for all my birthdays as a child, but I do remember all the trips and experiences we shared as a family. As a father who, at the beginning of my career and to this day, still regret not spending more time with my boys, my passion now is planning excursions for us as a family. It does not matter if it's a day trip or a weeklong trip, quality time together is what's important to our family and me. We love talking about our trips and the fun we've had.

In the early days, I missed some important moments. I didn't realize that I could have my career and support my family at the same time. I learned to do both, I must make sure the company I work for has the same goals that I have. That realization led me to find a great company, The JPI Group. The owner and president, Yom and Paul Douglass, have created a family-oriented culture. Whatever you do in life, find a place of employment that shares your values and goals. Yes, it may affect you financially, but true wealth lies in the mental and emotional well-being that comes from strong families. Families that are present and available for one another.

Being able to make our kid's events was priceless. The events provided many opportunities to teach life lessons, and I was thankful to be present and available to go through these teachable moments with them. It was always exciting, having fun and performing well during the good times. But when they lost, the performance did not go well, or they were cut from a team, some of the tough conversations also become the most meaningful ones. Often when young kids lose a game, they may be upset for a few minutes, but ten minutes later, they're playing with friends and on to the next. But as they get older, they feel like they've let their team down and sometimes want to quit. Being able to talk to my kids about failure and understanding the only thing unacceptable about failure is not getting up again was priceless. Helping them "in the moment" to overcome failure, teaching them that failure is not a bad thing, they are not a bad person, building their character, and teaching them how hard and consistently you must work to be successful - that's what fatherhood is about. The tough conversations were the ones I enjoyed most.

My oldest son did not make the 7th-grade basketball team, and it was a tough night. We talked about what it takes to be successful, and his work over the next year was unbelievable. He made the 8th-grade basketball team and never looked back. Now, if something does not go right, it still hurts, but he understands the sun is going to rise tomorrow, and he must keep working. My youngest son, Jaylen, did not make the summer league soccer team, and it was his first time being cut. He was upset and embarrassed. Sometimes failure is a good motivator. We taught our boys that when they prepare and give their all, there is no need for embarrassment. We explained to Jaylen that he would need to work hard to prepare for the next year's tryouts. He made the elite team this summer, and we are so proud of him.

Allowing your kids to fail is not a bad thing. They must understand that everything will not be perfect. This is life, and learning this is okay. Talking to your kids and helping them through these moments is so important. After a loss, we always discuss what they learned and how they can become better.

It has also been good for my boys to hear about some of my failures, not only with sports but also in my personal life, school, and work. Kids see their parents as perfect a lot of times in their eyes. When you explain to them your struggles and obstacles, they appreciate it. It makes you approachable, human, and relatable and teaches the importance of growth. It gives them the freedom to express their feelings. Sometimes it's difficult to talk about your failures to your kids, but in the long run, it's good to express how it affected you and what you learned. My kids enjoyed hearing about the struggles my wife and I had in high school and college. At first, I was embarrassed, but then I remembered how far we have come and how the Lord has blessed us. Those conversations with our kids have opened their minds to trying different things, from playing an instrument to taking roles in plays, different sports, and other activities. They understand failure is okay; just give your best and learn; perfection is not a requirement. My wife and I never want our kids to be afraid to try something because of fear of failing. We have discussed how many things we did not try because of that fear and how much we regret not trying when we were younger. At least we would have the satisfaction of knowing we tried, and it simply did not work out.

I have learned many lessons from my kids as a coach. I grew up in an era where coaches encouraged you by yelling, screaming, and punishing you when you messed up. I had the opportunity to coach both of my son's basketball teams. My kids taught me that you must have patience as a coach, and a lot of times, kids struggle or mess up because they are afraid to let their parents down, nervous, not sure what to do, or were never coached on what to do. When you are a coach, you are also a mentor, teacher, and sometimes a father figure. Kids want to be loved and know that no matter what happens, you will love them even if they fail or lose. As a coach, remember you don't know what a child is going through, and your interaction with them may be the only positive, validating, or encouraging part of their day.

My wife and I have honest conversations with our kids. We want them to understand that life is a roller coaster ride, but they do not have to go through it alone. We are here to help them navigate this adventure.

Raising two Black boys has led to an entirely different conversation as they have become teenagers. Our oldest is going to college and has been driving, and with all the social injustices that have occurred, we have had some tough conversations. We've explained to our son the importance of how he must handle himself when he is pulled over or during an encounter with the police. We've told him, "Obey their orders so you can come home." I heard Maria Taylor repeat her father's words, "comply or die," which I've also repeated to my son regularly. This is a necessary conversation Black fathers are having, and it's something Black fathers worry about every day. Kids are a sponge, and with social media, there are times you are unaware of what they're learning or having conversations with their friends about. I want to make sure my sons understand they can speak with me about anything. There is a thin line because I am their father, not their friend, and that line can be tricky.

My childhood was not perfect, but it was the foundation that turned me into the man I am today. Many things I saw as a child have stuck with me to this day, the good and bad. It is a reminder to me and all fathers that when spending time with our families, kids are always watching and learning. Be aware of your surroundings and how you respond in certain situations because that is how your kids will respond. No matter what we say, kids emulate their parent's actions, both good and bad. I try to remind my kids they are going to be in situations throughout life, but how they respond will be the determining factor. Dr. Martin Luther King, Jr. said, "The ultimate measure of a man is not where he stands in moments of comfort and convenience, but where he stands at times of challenge and controversy." This is something I am still learning and trying to improve on every day.

Yes, being a father is one of the greatest things in the world. There is no perfect way to be a father, but most importantly, we must be there for our kids. The quality time I have spent with my family has helped me develop a close relationship with my boys. The pandemic was not a great experience for any of us, but it allowed all of us to slow down and reflect on what's most important in life - God and family.

Spend quality time with your family and loved ones as much as possible and cherish those moments.

Kenneth Swan, Jr.

Kenneth Swan is a retired Army Veteran of 23 years. He has been married to his wife, Takosha Swan, for ten years and is a father to a teenage daughter, an 8-year-old son, and a 6-year-old daughter. He is originally from the north side of Houston, where he was raised until he enlisted in the military. He obtained a Bachelor's degree from Liberty University during his time in the military and was ordained as a minister by the late Pastor Sylvester Moore in 2013. In the military, he served multiple leadership roles in the medical field and recruiting. He was selected for the rank of Sergeant Major promotable and decided to retire to spend more time with his family. Kenneth now resides in Georgia with this family.

Chapter 15

A Letter to my Younger Self: Fathers Show Up

Kenneth Swan, Jr.

I always knew I wanted to get married and have a family. I was raised in a two-parent household with two younger siblings, living a life many family members didn't have but desired. There are many things my father had to put up with while raising me and my sisters that I had long forgotten. Most of the time, I just remember the good things I did, and I thought all the bad was from my sisters. My father would always say, "Boy, you see all the hell you put me through? Just remember it will be coming back double to you when you have your children." I know he wasn't trying to wish bad things on me, but many believe this saying. I remember  telling my father, "No, it's not; I'll change something so that I won't have to endure what you had to put up with, Dad."

The Early Years: Winging It

It wasn't by accident or planned pregnancy when I became a father. See, I became a father when I married into a package deal. My oldest daughter was already six years old and full of life when I entered the picture and began dating her mother.

Her mother did her best to provide and care for her daughter as a single parent, as her daughter's biological father was not consistently active in her life. He was not a man of his word and would show up now and then, and her mother and I knew that did not make her happy. It is one thing to have a father who is never present, but I witnessed firsthand the hurt a child experiences when let down by a father who makes promises but doesn't follow through.

During the dating phases with her mother, I didn't spend much time getting to know my future daughter personally. I later realized I was only exposed to glimpses of who she was and what she needed during that time. In my eyes, she could do no wrong until I began noticing her do things I didn't like but didn't seem to bother her mom. Unfortunately, I mistakenly overlooked those things during the honeymoon phase of my relationship with her mother. Instead, I brushed it off as her being young and believed she would change once I was fully in her life.

As a person who only had to be concerned about himself for a long time, once married, I had to invest myself in my wife and a child, and it was not as easy as I expected. With our daughter, it became my responsibility to fill a void I didn't understand. Nor did I fathom that void would challenge our relationship even to this present day. Like many stepfathers, the challenge for me, who was present daily, became parenting with the obstacle of a pop-up dad who was not there for the everyday challenges and attitudes of raising their child. My daughter would later tell me that her biological father's inconsistency caused her resentment towards me because of what she wanted from her biological father. I had no idea.

I remember one of my military friends saying, "I respect you for raising your stepdaughter and being there for her. That's commendable." I said, "No big deal," because it was in my heart to love, support, and raise her from the beginning. What I didn't realize were the obstacles that awaited me. I later understood why he was praising me.

Many times I have thought, *what did I get myself into?* All I wanted was to help raise her until she would launch into the world and be a productive human being. It wasn't until later in the relationship that I began to understand how important it was for my daughter also to have love and support from her biological father. Before I stepped into the role of a father, I didn't fully understand the building and bonding process of a father-daughter relationship. Let me explain.

When I was a child, I remember doing what my parents told me to do when they told me to do it. I remember being obedient (most of the time), respectful, and all that stuff, which I assumed was automatic for all children. I didn't consider that my father had a six-year head start on instilling his principles, morals, and standards into me compared to my fatherhood starting six years into my daughter's life. In my mind, I believed things would fall into place for my new family if I were present. My intentions were honorable, but my execution was off, and I didn't understand.

From the beginning, I 'winged it' regarding what discipline my wife supported, which made it difficult for me. My upbringing was the only frame of reference for raising a child, and I relied on it to structure my home. My wife was raised by her biological mother and stepfather, an entirely different example and set of rules to enforce discipline compared to my example. Her stepfather also came into her life at an early age.

Early in our marriage, my wife suddenly changed, becoming increasingly protective whenever I disciplined or spoke firmly to our daughter. My wife would fly into the conversations to rescue her from me as if I were "the bad guy." I believed it limited the support I had with fathering our daughter. My wife and I would talk about it, but I was left with the notion that I needed to change my perspective and approach to disciplining our daughter. These conversations would leave me feeling disrespected and angry because I was trying to guide her in the right direction. Years later, my wife finally opened up to me about an occasion when I had gotten angry with our daughter and said something she didn't like. From that time forward, my wife felt she needed to protect our daughter from me. It bothered me deeply that she had used one moment in time to make a decision that lasted for years. The protection she provided for our daughter challenged my guidance in most of the affairs concerning our daughter, which extended from our home to school to whatever our daughter was doing.

Looking back, I realize that I became stricter with my corrections because I felt our daughter was getting away with no consequences.

This mindset is what I believe helped foster resentment in my relationship with our daughter. We would spend time together as a family, but I didn't spend one-on-one quality time with my daughter. Over the years, a wall developed between my daughter and me. I tried to step back and be more optimistic with her. I would let my guard down and try to be more easygoing with her, but it did not change how we interacted with one another for the better. As she grew older, I increasingly saw the lack of respect and obedience filtering into school and around family members and friends, the very behavior that I tried to prevent early on by holding her accountable.

My wife and I have talked about how she was raised and her relationship with her stepfather. She didn't like things concerning his methods, which influenced her views on my interactions with our daughter. Our conversation consisted of her saying, "We don't have to raise our children as our parents raised us." I will not lie and say I wasn't angry or upset with some of my father's methods of raising me, but I would not change anything because it made me the person I am today.

If a child doesn't have consistency from both parents being on the same page, they will flow toward the least resistance and reject anything that doesn't align with their selfish desires. I remember having a conversation with my daughter that went like this, "Dad, why do you keep bothering me about cleaning my room? You are always getting on me about the same thing." My response was, "It's my job to keep at you until you're doing it yourself." My mindset is to stay on you until you take responsibility for your actions. Needless to say, that went in one ear and out the other because even today, she still needs attention in this area. There have been many things I would have loved to share with our daughter concerning life, but I believe when a child thinks they know what's best concerning unknown aspects of their life, then going through life issues will become their master teacher. Whenever my father was redirecting me after I made mistakes, he would say, "You don't have to like me or love me, that's not what I'm here for, but I will do my job and raise you." His words have stuck with me through the years, but I have only recently understood the seriousness of his statement and the stance he was making.

The Blended Family: Real Talk

I have struggled for years and didn't recognize that I was falling short as a father because of a lack of consistent boundaries and foundational structure that I failed to discuss and implement early in my relationship with my daughter. Unfortunately, this started to spill into me raising my two younger children as well.

Early on, I placed the responsibility for our daughter on my wife because I didn't understand my role as a father. As I later opened myself up to growth, I recently understood that my daughter didn't have a father role model in her life before me, yet I expected her to know how to interact with and respect me as a father. My teenage daughter had to help me understand that she needed me not just as a disciplinary protector but also to check in on her wellbeing. Not just asking how you are feeling or doing today, but keeping an open dialogue so she would feel free to share her issues without judgment. To be happy for her in the things that make her happy. Look beyond the results of her actions to understand the *why* of her actions. My wife has helped me be in the moment with our kids because they grow up fast. I'm learning to allow them to make mistakes without my judgmental expectations. Every generation has its challenges. It may seem trivial to the senior generation, but it could mean life or death to the child going through it. I now understand that I must always be vigilant regarding recognizing my child's state. Because of the lessons learned from my relationship with my daughter, I better understand what I need to do as a father to my younger children.

One of the most critical conversations my wife and I didn't have before marriage was how we would discipline our daughter and support one another in raising her. If communicated ahead of time, I believe this conversation could have eliminated plenty of heartache and drama from our life. Respect, discipline, and order were non-negotiables during my upbringing. The desired outcome was guaranteed. There were no options. I am not saying my parents abused us, but they didn't let things go easily. We received whoppings. What the new generation calls *going into the corner for a time out* was *facing the wall* spent on your knees for an extended period in our parent's hallway during my childhood. We were restricted to our rooms and given no TV privileges as a consequence of disobedience.

So, to say raising a child you didn't birth is a challenge would be an understatement for me. It has been one of the most challenging tasks of my life, realizing I can only truly give what is supported and understood by my wife because of the blended family dynamics.

There have been moments in my life as a father when I thought, *look what you have gotten yourself into trying to raise these children.* I felt it was too hard, and I questioned why I had to put up with this. Honestly, I didn't want to be a father at those moments. But when I thought about my father and how he had the choice before I was born to abort or walk away, and he chose to be present in my life, it continually gives me the right heart and motivation to be here for my children.

From this father's perspective, mothers play one of the most crucial roles in a blended family. They are the connector that sets the tone of positive or negative energy and respect within the union. I believe a future blended family needs to have important conversations before marriage on how the dynamics of having two fathers in their life will work. A stepfather's respect level from a child is based on the love and respect level the mother establishes from the beginning. The child needs to understand their future parent intends to help raise and take care of them like they were their biological child and that they will be treated with love and respect. The child should also be reassured that the stepfather is not trying to take their biological father's place and is committed to being a pillar and strength they can depend on for guidance and support. I believe it is important that the mother understands the same, that the future father's love will be unconditional for their child, and they can trust him with their child's life.

The advice I would give to my younger self is don't allow negative interactions to distort how you feel about interacting and communicating with your child. In other words, remember your child is just that, a child who needs help to develop understanding and maturity about life. It is vital to address the little things in a way that will facilitate growth, rather than division, in the father-child relationship. Children have concerns, questions, and opinions about things they experience in life, and we are responsible for allowing them to express themselves in a safe environment of love. We may disagree with them, but it doesn't hurt to listen and give guidance. I would advise all future fathers to let the child know at the beginning that there will always be an open door for them to communicate with you and that we will work it out together no matter what.

I would advise all fathers to have regular family meetings to discuss family business and issues that will help to create opportunities for each family member to express themselves and show that all voices in the house deserve to be heard and acknowledged. As fathers, we must understand that relationships with our children take constant work and regular maintenance. It is not a one-time fix or trade-in type of relationship when it doesn't work the way we want. Our children need our patience and commitment to show up daily as their fathers, no matter the weather in the house that day. Fathers make hard sacrifices for the greater good of the family.

I wish more men or fathers would have been there to check in on me as a father. I often felt alone and powerless in situations I know others have made it through. Fathers' feelings are often neglected because we are considered the strong ones and don't need all that sensitive, emotional talking about our feelings. Well, I'm here to say that's a LIE. Because of our responsibilities, we must be more sensitive as fathers to keep our mental and emotional states intact. It is in my heart to check on other fathers to let them know they are not alone and that there is light on the other side of their efforts and love.

I have not given up on raising my children. I believe they will understand the *whys* of all I have done as a father as they grow and experience life. I will continue to do the best I can with what God has given into my hands. Like the Bible says in Proverbs 22:6, *" Train a child in the way he should go, and when he is old, he will not depart from it. "*

Change Must Start With Me

I'm so thankful to God for leading me to seek help and guidance to evaluate my mindset and actions as a father to become better. All I know is what I know. I have been helped tremendously by opening up to those I trust and respect who have exemplified wisdom with their children.

In the Bible, there are many passages about respecting and honoring your parents. There was a disconnect for me in my home that I had to face before the environment could change. Recognizing and acknowledging the disconnect has allowed me to see my tendency to subconsciously transfer my hurt and disappointments through harsh interactions with my children. I didn't realize that I was carrying this baggage. I learned that I had to forgive my father for his words that affected my self-esteem and his actions that caused me to have an unhealthy fear of authority. This revelation alone has affected me in so many areas of my life.

As a father, I wanted to be looked at with respect, not understanding that I was not truly respecting myself first. I could not receive what I didn't believe about myself. The highest form of respect for myself is revealed by what I choose to allow in my life. My life lacked the driving forces of consistency and discipline. Many would probably say, "You were in the military; you definitely have discipline." The military was a system of repetitious actions that allowed a person to exemplify discipline and consistency. It's easy to hide behind systems that work, but what you do when no one is around is what determines your actual level of discipline and consistency. These systems were a method of surviving life, not thriving in it.

I am working on myself to create a new life by respecting the most important person in my life, and that is me. As a person and father, I have learned that giving what you do not have is impossible. As fathers, we must cultivate an environment for the harvest we want and pull up the weeds that block us from being our best. We protect and nurture our families, but that doesn't solely mean protecting them from outside physical harm from the world. It also means protecting our kids and families from our past mental, emotional, and psychological disappointments and hurts by confronting them rather than transferring them.

Renewed Understanding and Commitment

My father was not raised by his biological father, who he only met twice in his life. He was raised by a stepfather that didn't treat him with the love and respect he deserved as a son. He had men in his life that were examples of "how not to be a father." However, he tried his best to show up and be present in my life as best as he could. He made mistakes along the way, but he did show up. I am extremely grateful for all my father (Kenneth Swan Sr.) did and sacrificed for his family. I love and appreciate him more every day as I better understand fatherhood.

Fatherhood is an investment into a destiny that may not pay off until the next generation, but I choose to remain committed.

I have chosen to show up and be present in my children's lives as the best person and father I can be. I have made mistakes, but as long as there is breath in my body, I will continue to grow to be the best father I can be. This father will create and maintain boundaries that align with my values, respect myself, and know my value in my home as a father. I pray today that more fathers will show up and be positively present and purposefully active in their children's lives; that each day our homes, communities, and the world become healthier, stronger, and better places for all of us to live.

C. Derek Easterling

Derek Easterling is currently serving in his second four-year term as Mayor of City of Kennesaw and is responsible for the efficient and orderly administration of city affairs.

Civic and community involvement is important to Derek. He is active in school system support activities where he has served as President of the Parent Teacher Student Association and is currently in his sixth year as a teacher in the state's third largest school district. He taught Leadership and Social Studies in middle school and now serves as the Senior Naval Science Officer at North Cobb High School. He also coached baseball for the Kennesaw Baseball Association for more than a decade.

Derek Easterling is originally from Fort Lauderdale, Florida. He enlisted in the U.S. Navy in 1980 where he rapidly advanced his career. In 1990, he was selected for the Naval Officer Indoctrination Course and attained the rank of Lieutenant completing his service through an early retirement option in December 1996. His decorations include the Defense Meritorious Service Medal, Joint Service Commendation Medal, Navy Commendation Medal, and the Navy Achievement Medal. During his time in service, he served aboard two fast-attack submarines, a submarine tender, an aircraft carrier, a special warfare unit, two North Atlantic Treaty Organization Commands, and at the U.S. Naval Academy. He has lived and worked all over the United States, its territories, and throughout Europe.

Following his Navy retirement, Derek spent the next two years traveling around the United States working in a variety of jobs outside of a normal career path hoping to discover what would be next. He moved to North Georgia in 1999, to work in the family business where he designed and built furniture and cabinetry. In 2003, Derek completed law enforcement officer training and joined the Cobb County Sheriff's Office as a Deputy Sheriff where he served until 2010. He relocated to Tampa in 2010, to care for an aging parent where he accepted a position as a Hillsborough County School District Field Inspector. In 2012, he returned to Georgia and was employed as Security Supervisor for Kennestone WellStar Hospital until April of 2015.

Derek holds a Bachelor of Science in Sports Management and a Master of Education Secondary Education in History.

Derek and his wife Dawn have been married for 17 years.

"As I face new challenges in my life, I need to keep pushing forward, learning, being, and doing – I am in a battle with myself to become the man my wife and children think I am. It is not about me; it is about giving back and doing the right thing, always. I want to be the best version of myself, and I want to make a difference!"

CHAPTER 16

Rethinking Fatherhood

C. Derek Easterling

Pop's Home

I caught a glimpse of my dad's car in the driveway as the bus driver turned left and proceeded down the narrow two-lane road past our house. As soon as the bus stopped and the driver opened the door, I was off and running. It had to be something special; my dad was never home this early. As I ran through the front door, I saw him sitting in his reclining chair, leaning forward with his arms folded across his chest, and I stopped dead in my tracks. "So, do you want to tell me what happened at the bus stop this morning before you went to school?" I knew from his demeanor he  was not asking. Inside my head, I heard myself say, "Holy ****! He came home early from work for this?"

My dad was tough! He was tough on himself, and he was tough on me. It was clear that he was not my friend; he was the boss of me, the prosecutor, judge, jury, and enforcer, and he could cover it all in less than five seconds. But he was my hero, too. There was nothing in this world that my dad could not do or fix. He was cool. He walked with a slight swagger, and he always stood a little taller when my mom was around. There was never any doubt that dad loved her, my two younger sisters, or me. He worked 12-16 hours a day, seven days a week, to make ends meet. He made it to extra-curricular activities and sporting events for each of us, not always on time but on his time. He cheered and guided each of his three children through adolescence and into adulthood the best way he knew how. My dad has been Father of the Year each year since I can remember. He is the model man and father that I wanted to become.

My journey of fatherhood has been complicated and guilt-ridden. Because of this, I have opted to share my perspective as a stepfather. I know I do not have to emphasize that my perspective is one side of the story, but I assure you, it is my truth.

First, I need you to understand that fatherhood is an honor, privilege, and rite of passage in my world, where I am king and ruler. Fatherhood is something you aspire to and a journey you commit yourself to complete, despite the challenges and obstacles faced. There are no textbooks or manuals. There are a few good men with great advice and counsel, and for sure, a thousand critics are ready to tell you what you should or should not have done, including me. When I compare the abilities and actions of fathers, I compare them to those of my father. Pop, as I call him, set the standard by which I measure the totality of my actions and achievements as a father and in life. If anyone should write about the qualities of an effective father, it is Pop.

When I talked with Pop about this fatherhood project, asking for his thoughts, opinions, and advice, he leaned back in his chair, took a deep breath in, and ran the palm of his hand across the top of his head; he remained still and silent for a minute or two. As usual, when he spoke, his response was shocking and simple: "Good order, discipline, forgiveness, understanding, and time. Stay in the fight and be the parent."

Children do not want you to be their best friend. They want you to guide and protect them through their childhood. Teach them how to stand on their own two feet and accept responsibility for their decisions and who they are. If you do nothing else, be present in their daily life! These are the lessons I learned from my father.

Not a scientific study by any stretch of the imagination, but I reached out to six successful fathers and ten children of upstanding fathers to identify commonalities in style or individual traits. The same two questions were used for each group. I know each of the men I spoke with. I interviewed children of fathers I know, many of whom I have known for some time or had as students. Remember, this is not a scientific study but was used to support what I have observed in other fathers:

Father

- What are three principles or character traits you would say every father needs to be effective in his role as a father?

- What was the most challenging aspect or phase of fatherhood for you?

Children

- What are the three-character traits you think a man needs to be a great father?

- What makes your father a great father?

Overwhelmingly, the fathers believed being committed to providing for their family was the priority and took precedence over everything involving their children, including spending a lot of time with them. However, these fathers were all over the board in listing the principles or character traits needed to be a good father. Responses included compassion, having a great sense of humor, empathy, consistency, kindness, being a good listener, etcetera.

The children all agreed that having a father present and engaged in their lives made a positive difference in who they are today. The responses that sold me on the value of having a dad around stated their father's presence overshadowed the absences and "he made his time count" when he was present. I can attest to this in my life while growing up. When my dad was around, everything was better.

I have also spoken with men raised by their mother or grandmother, who never knew or had no relationship with their father, and turned out to be excellent fathers with exceptional children. I singled out one of these fathers to highlight his responses. His "must-have" character traits to be a good father include the ability to provide, set a good example, and respect for God. Last, he says, "Make no excuses; it is a journey!"

As a Senior Naval Science Instructor (teacher), I can attest to the significance and positive effect of setting an example for our students and our children. We have been working together for two years, and I hear, feel, and see the effort we put into our students every school day and most days during the summer. Most of our students, all Naval Junior Reserve Officer Training Corps (NJROTC) cadets, practice, train, attend leadership programs, classes, and camps, and frequently hang out with us throughout the summer. These kids, not unlike our children, want to be around people they feel safe or comfortable with, and our classrooms provide just such an environment for them. The best action we can take is to be role models for these young folks to emulate. Good order and discipline encapsulate the NJROTC program, along with honor, courage, and commitment. Ephesians 6:4 states, "Fathers, do not provoke your children to anger, but bring them up in the discipline and instruction of the Lord." In my studies, I understand this to mean guiding your children gently through the process with constructive criticism and teaching responsibility. As NJROTC instructors, we do not have all the answers, but we make a difference by putting forth the effort for each of our students. We put ourselves out there daily and share our stories, successes, and failures. We push hard to instill a desire to be better at whatever they do, and we demonstrate how to serve one another and the community to make a positive difference through our actions. Likewise, as we also "walk the talk" in front of our children, we have the same positive effect on them.

It is crucial that our children not hear us make excuses. Instead, we must accept responsibility for our actions (or inaction) and deal with the consequences. We must OWN IT! I am not proud of every decision I have made. I have made wise decisions, some decisions that made no difference, and some poor choices along life's journey, but not one defines me. Instead, I am best defined by how I have responded and the totality of my choices. NO EXCUSES!

A Mid-Life Journey

I did not know the joy and heartbreak of being a father in my twenties or early thirties. However, I began my father-like journey at 45 when I fell deeply in love with a woman who had four children between 18 months and nine years old. We became good friends, and we talked at work about our lives, her children, and our individual dreams. Then it happened… It has been 17 years since we took our friendship to the next level and 16 since we said, "I will," and "I do." Do not think for one minute my age provided any advantages or "fatherly" wisdom to take on my new role. In fact, my age required greater effort to understand and accept the changes in my new role, my standard of living, and my lifestyle. Keeping up with a family of six, learning each child and their individual likes and dislikes, learning carpool etiquette, school, and nap schedules, eating habits, who all the Disney princesses are, coaching, and still working one full-time job and two part-time jobs were no small feat. What was I thinking? Somehow, we made it work. I survived countless episodes of *Teletubbies*, *Barney*, *Full House*, and *Reba* reruns, recognized most of the Disney princesses on sight, and can prepare a supper that brings everyone to the table. I do not know that I did any of this well. I only know I put my best foot forward and made the effort to be successful.

It was rarely smooth sailing for us. There were challenges contested in court regarding visitation, who can and cannot drop the children off or pick them up, when and where, how long, whose holiday is what, and more. But we persevered or tried, anyway. At 11, the oldest moved in with her dad. It was her choice, and to this day, I still do not know why or how we let this happen. The younger three have lived with us the entire time. The dynamics of our home have three different takes, one for each child:

Oldest: Mom—is everything.

           Stepfather—that person Mom married

           Responsibilities—protect Mom from stepfather (me)

Middle: Mom—is everything and makes everything happen

           Stepfather—coach when my friends and I play ball; my mechanic when something in my car does not work or needs repair; my homework helper, annoyer—"why are you bothering me" (for the first two days back home after a long visit with dad)

Responsibilities—tell my biological father everything

Youngest: Mom—transportation and Starbucks run buddy

Stepfather—everything else

Responsibilities—get my older sister to move out and my big brother to move on

Who Am I

Like my dad, I am tough and a little rough around the edges. I work long and hard every day of the week, and I have ever since I can remember. Work is more than a paycheck or an obligation; it is who I am, the place I go to escape my reality and the issues at hand. If only I could work a little longer, I could fix all my problems.

I never figured on being married with children when I retired from the Navy, especially not at my age. I was not prepared financially to have children, and I certainly was not prepared for the unnecessary challenges thrown in front of me by my wife's ex and her children. But I love my wife, and I promised her I would make the effort, and I have kept my promise to her. Most everyone who knew me said I would not make it more than a year or two with the turmoil and pressure of raising someone else's children. Most everyone else, especially the ex-husband's family, waited for me to be what they assumed I was—a mean, loud, set-in-his-ways old man. But I entered this marriage and family with determination and a newfound purpose. My goal was not to prove everyone wrong but to prove to myself I could love someone else the way they deserved to be loved.

It is at this point in my story I need to acknowledge this is not my first or even my second marriage, but it is my last. I now understand what commitment means and how difficult the challenges of marriage and family are, especially if you want it to work. It took me longer than most to realize mutual and individual responsibilities exist in a relationship and communicating with your other half is essential to the success of that relationship. I was so focused on my career and had an excuse phrase (short-term sacrifice for a long-term gain) which I used to preclude myself from talking about problems in the relationship.

Being married with children required me to know and understand the role I played in the family dynamics. I mean, you cannot be everything to everyone, but you can be present when they need you the most. Let me also say, it is difficult going through every day trying to be perfect. There is no margin for error; they are watching you every step of the way, just hoping to catch you doing or saying something wrong so they can tell everyone how right they were and wrong you are in the moment.

Three Basic Rules

We have all heard it said there are three sides to every story: his side, her side, and the truth. With only this little tidbit as background, let me lay out a few suggested ground rules for blended families:

- Do not tell the children the truth about why Mommy and Daddy could not live together any longer. As a parent, only telling one side of a story is skewed, biased, or simply untruthful information. Tell the story long and often enough, and the children will believe the story too. Divorce or separation is difficult enough for adults, and deciding who to believe is even tougher for the children. Besides, they will figure it out for themselves.

- Do not discuss child support with or around the children. It is a legal matter and an "adult-only" topic. We should never cause children to feel guilty because of the cost of raising them. Nor should they feel blame or shame for the cost of child support. After 17 years of fatherhood, I can say with authority the cost of raising a child goes far beyond money. It is money, time, patience, sacrifice, nurturing, correcting, mentoring, joy, heartbreak, blood, sweat, tears, and so much more. There is no hero here. Every parent, whether custodial, stepparent, or non-custodial, despite your individual and combined imperfections, should be all in, no matter the cost!

- Do not act like your shit does not stink. We all make mistakes; that is how we learn, and it is simply referred to as learning the ropes or gaining experience. Do the hard and dirty but necessary work of facing yourself in the mirror and do whatever is necessary to get it right.

- Remember, the stepparent is helping to raise your children. They do not want credit for it. They have committed to their spouse and the children. Co-parenting is not easy. It can even get ugly. But the reality is you are all here, and the stepparent is also on the starting and finishing team. Like it or not, figuring it out for the good of the children is the only option and must be the priority. I have simply wanted us both to be the men we should be, for the children's sake.

- Keep adult arguments, dislikes, fights, lies, and drama between the parents. The children should not be privy to these discussions or after-discussion commentary. This new and challenging terrain of co-parenting is difficult for adults to navigate. Imagine the emotions the children must be feeling, both spoken and unspoken. The last thing they need is the added stress and confusion of fighting and angry parents. It is the last thing any of you need.

Okay, so that was harsh but truthful. My first seventeen years as a parent would have been much easier if the parents could have learned how to get along and communicate. After all, we want the same thing for our children—the opportunity to learn, laugh, and love in a comfortable and safe home.

Forget the Rules

BE NICE TO EACH OTHER! The kids are watching and learning from you. I experienced the near horror of my youngest stepdaughter mimicking me one day. Leadership lesson number one: You do not have control over what happens to you, but you have one hundred percent control over how you respond.

Believe me, your kids are watching and listening closely! They are also learning the behavior to expect from you in similar situations. Your responses become who you are to them. And man-oh-man did I ever have to work at changing my response behavior! Consider the classroom teacher who was conducting a response-relationship-association lesson. She showed her class a picture of a traffic signal with the red-light activated and asked, what does a red signal indicate? Her student, Sarah, responded that it means to stop. When she showed the class a picture of the same traffic signal with a green light, the teacher asked Johnny what it meant, and he responded by saying, "Go dammit, GO!" Yes, our children are watching and modeling what they see and hear from us.

I love my wife and would do anything for her, but I changed the way I respond because I love my children. The first time your precious little girl kicks her feet into the ground and says, "Are you kidding me?!" with perfect sarcastic intonation is enough to make anyone want to respond better. Although I will admit when she was not watching, I laughed a little at her reaction.

No excuses...

I was too harsh, too cut and dry, too black and white; there was no gray area in my life. Well, at least my life was that way before children. Good order and discipline, neatness, organization, and being prompt are fundamental characteristics of daily living. But life and the family component are not so rigid. Responsibilities may be well-defined, but you must remain flexible to survive life's journey.

My greatest success as a father is also my greatest failure. I gave all my children the same start, the same opportunity to learn, grow, and be successful. However, not all my children learned the lesson the way I wanted them to learn it. As the children grew, the older two at home preferred to ignore and not engage in conversation with me.

Questions about how their day was or what they were up to this weekend were increasingly met with the conversation ending with "okay" or "nothing really" responses. Over time, callousness crept in, and I withdrew from some interactions with the older children. I quit giving hugs and saying, "I love you." I still love my children; I just did not say it aloud.

Biological fathers: If your children do not live with you and their mom is married to another man who will help, do not be disparaging toward the stepfather.

Stepfathers: Never ever say anything bad or degrading about the child's biological father. He will always be their father!

For both of you: Be the bigger man in all situations and under all circumstances. You will accomplish nothing by bringing each other down except to create more tension and hurt. Be empathetic and forgiving; your children will benefit more from these actions.

Fatherhood Checklist

- Kindhearted

- Thick-skinned

- Grateful

- Gentle

- Rough around the edges

- Flexible

- Committed

- Determined

- Rigid

- Focused

- Distracted

- Compassionate

- ~~Heartless~~

- Direct

- Harsh

- On-time

- Proactive

- Interactive

- Demonstrate a willingness to learn.

- Be you and go with it. If it works, great; if not, try it differently.

- Give everything; expect nothing in return.

- Most importantly, make the effort to be the man God intends for you to be.

Give everything; expect nothing in return.

Okay, so my fatherhood checklist is an attempt to be funny or poke fun at me and my thought process of being a good father. On any day, I have been none or all of them. The fact is, I have spent the past 17 years attempting to be a better husband, father, friend, teacher, leader, and man of God. I do not always win the battle, but I am currently in the lead, AND I will continue to make the effort to be the best version of myself for those that I love and care for the most.

Rethinking Fatherhood

Fathers keep pushing. Keep making the effort. One day, your children will get it, and they will love you for it! Stand up against the naysayers, stand up for your family, for your country, and your God. Believe in yourself and what you are doing. Be the parent, not your child's best friend! Be firm but fair. Be there for them! You may not feel you are making a difference, but you are. The value of making the effort is immeasurable. The positive difference you are making in your children's lives carries over to their friends and then their friends' interactions, and so on. It is an exponential force and a force of change. It will amaze you how much your child will learn from you during their childhood.

"When I was a boy of 14, my father was so ignorant I could hardly stand to have the old man around. But when I got to be 21, I was astonished at how much the old man had learned in seven years."

~ Mark Twain

... ***ABOUT THAT MORNING AT THE BUS STOP***. I was by no stretch of the imagination a big kid in the sixth grade. I was wiry, not even skinny, but wiry. Well, there was this eighth-grader who insisted on bullying me at the bus stop each morning. I had cried to my dad one too many times about this kid's actions. Pop did not want to hear anything else about it and told me if I did nothing about it, I would grow up without a backbone (he did not use the word backbone), but I completely understood what he was saying.

The next morning, just like clockwork, I showed up at the bus stop and waited. My little sisters rode by on their bicycles when they suddenly halted in the middle of the street, dropped their bicycles, and came running toward me, crying. The bully had spit on one of them. I cleaned the front of her dress with my handkerchief (yes, I carried one until the day I graduated high school) and sent her on her way. The bully turned toward me, laughed, and said, "What are you going to do about it, you little ***** (expletive)?!"

He did not see it coming. The first punch knocked him backward, and the second one sent him to the ground. I hit him every time he tried to stand up until he just sat there whimpering. When the bus arrived, everyone except this kid hurried to get on the bus, and for the first time in my middle school life, I sat in the seat by myself. There was no one in the seat in front of, behind, or beside me. I had taken a stand and reveled in my victory.

Pop listened to my story intently, verified the "facts" with my sisters, and then spoke to the police when they knocked on our front door. I just knew I was in for an ass whooping for fighting, but as Pop stood up to walk away, he said, "Thanks for standing up for yourself and your sisters today." Fathers, stand up for what you believe in and what you believe is just and right. Be the man God wants you to be.

Kevin Montgomery

Kevin Montgomery, a native of Washington, D.C., was raised in Prince George's County, Maryland. He earned his Bachelor of Arts degree in Sociology from Norfolk State University, Norfolk, Virginia. He was commissioned in the United States Army as a 2nd Lieutenant in the Field Artillery Corps and transitioned to the Logistics Corps. His leadership abilities were forged and tried early in his career in support of Operation Iraqi Freedom in Baghdad, Iraq, during the reconstruction period. Throughout his military career, his positions increased in complexity as he focused on developing his knowledge and level of skill.

Kevin later took his talent to work for Caterpillar Inc. as an innovative supervisor, applying Six Sigma methodologies to complex challenges in machining, welding, maintenance, paint, and assembly process implementation and outcomes. He focused on maximizing efficiency and productivity at every opportunity, no matter the section of the value stream he led.

Answering the call to serve, Kevin volunteered to deploy during the expansion of forces in Operation Enduring Freedom, Kandahar, Afghanistan, and three years later in Amman, Jordan. His logistical intuitiveness supported half of the Afghanistan combat theater with strategic logistical support and, while in Jordan, planned for a possible U.S. presence in Syria.

Kevin's membership with Alpha Phi Alpha Fraternity has given him opportunities to serve communities around the world in addressing voting disparities through education, awareness, and male mentorship in the absence of qualified role models.

Kevin is the proud father of the charming Chance Ellington, an adventurous adolescent full of life, and he is the life partner to an ambitious and inspired Danielle Nicole.

They reside peacefully in Wisconsin.

CHAPTER 17

The Power of Perseverance

Kevin Montgomery

O n a "sanctified Sunday" at the Columbia Hospital for Women, Leslie and Kevin welcomed me, an eight-week premature baby boy who would call the Neonatal Intensive Care Unit (NICU) home, for the first few months after my birth. My mother attempted to have

a child before my birth, but her pregnancy resulted in a miscarriage, and she was told that she could not have children. I'm not sure why she could not bear children, but it's safe to assume that it was likely due to health reasons that contributed to my premature birth and illnesses to follow. I suffered fevers, fever blisters, and jaundice. In addition, my mother's post-birth ailments prevented her from breastfeeding, so wet nurses fed me for the first couple of weeks of my life. Nevertheless, I grew to be a healthy child.

My parents' relationship, however, was short-lived after my birth. I have early memories of the three of us living in a one-bedroom apartment in southeast Washington, D.C. Trenton Park was the first home I can recall. Also living in Trenton Park, at one point, were my mother's oldest sister (Donna) and my maternal grandmother (Mildred). These two women played a critical role in my rearing.

My maternal grandmother, Mildred, successfully reared five children after my grandfather left her without a high school diploma or a job. After seeking the help of both her family and my grandfather's family, my grandmother soon realized that being on her own—with the help of the federal assistance program—was the most consistent support she would receive. In addition, the housing projects and the welfare program would afford my grandmother temporary support to get on her feet. Before my birth, my grandmother was trained as a Certified Nurse Assistant (CNA) and worked at a school-based health center in northwest Washington, D.C. While working as a CNA, my grandmother petitioned the Washington, D.C. School Board requesting special permission to enroll in night school to earn her high school diploma— not to take the General Education Development (GED) Test. Her petition was approved! After being approved to attend night school in her early forties, Mildred faced the dilemma of getting from work to class daily, so she purchased her only car, a sky-blue Mercury Monarch. She worked as a CNA all day and went to school in the evenings until she achieved her goal.

The pictures of my grandmother getting her high school diploma are forever etched in my mind. Unknowingly, my grandmother would set the example and tone for every generation of her family to follow. Mildred reared a church pastor and social worker, a Norfolk Public Schools board member, an analyst for the U.S. Department of Housing and Urban Development (HUD), an Internal Revenue Service (IRS) Management Program Analysis–Team Leader (working exclusively for the Office of the President), a Vice President of Underwriting for State Farm Insurance, and a U.S. Army Major Human Resources Officer. It is safe to say that Mildred's perseverance paid off.

The first and only place I can recall my parents living together was our home at Trenton Park. Trenton Park Apartments were safe and affordable for those with a limited income. My mother had dropped out of school after the tenth grade. My parents started dating a couple of years prior. After working a myriad of jobs and passing her G.E.D. Test, she later enlisted in the Washington, D.C. National Guard. She was honorably discharged from the District of Columbia National Guard because of my reoccurring illnesses. My mother, too, would persevere! She soon began her 39-year career as a civil servant with the IRS, starting as a General Schedule-1 (GS-1). Money was tight as a GS-1, making less than six thousand dollars a year, and while my father had at least two cars, my mother relied on the public transportation system for her transportation needs until she could afford a car. She took three buses to get me to my sitter's house and then another bus to work, and repeated it all over again after getting off work. We have come a long way.

Sometimes, I am surprised by what I can remember from my childhood. I can clearly recall my parents getting into verbal and physical altercations. When I was younger, I often came to my father's defense, and my mother would put us both out of the house until things cooled off and they calmed down. My father studied automotive repair in high school and proved to be an excellent mechanic when he was not running the streets and doing things to support his drug habits.

However, my father's lifestyle and the tension in my parent's relationship ultimately led to their separation. They had been together for about ten years before calling it quits. My dad was my mother's date to her junior prom, and he was her first boyfriend when she gave birth to me at 21, but Dad was often unfaithful and had several affairs. My parents' tumultuous time together, coupled with my mother's childhood trauma, her troubled relationship with her father, and the stress of becoming a single mother, all led to my mother's depression and eventually reaching her breaking point. I remember sitting in the waiting room and doodling on legal-size paper while waiting for my mom to complete her therapy sessions. It would take years for my mother to find a healthy place in life where her depression would be manageable, but she finally got there.

Soon after their split, my dad moved ten hours away to the Atlanta Metropolitan Area, where he met and married Linda. As my mother was rising like a phoenix from the ashes of her depression, my dad's marriage to Linda was crashing like a plane without a pilot. Meanwhile, his criminal activity was soaring.

My mother must have been in a much better place because she allowed me to spend the summer with my dad and my stepmother, Linda. My dad maintained the vehicle fleet for a golf course in town. It was the only time I can recall my dad having a real job when I was a child. He and Linda lived in an apartment on a lake, perfect for my sense of adventure. But my father missed the opportunity for some tremendous father-son time during that summer. I recall trying to fish in the lake with a stick, string, and a safety pin. What did this kid from the DMV (District of Columbia/Maryland/Virginia area) know about fishing? Not a damn thing. And my father didn't help either. It was crazy the amount of freedom I had as a six-year-old boy. Times have truly changed. My son, Chance, has a watch that monitors his location and serves as a telephone with five essential pre-programmed phone numbers.

One day my dad and I went downtown, and he left me in the car asleep. I later woke up, got out of the car, and walked around until I found him. No one questioned why a six-year-old boy walked around town without an adult. But, again, times were different. We were lucky that I was safe, and my sense of adventure was fed.

Sometimes you see things you wish you could unsee. I remember it like it was yesterday. One evening, I recall having a headache, and my dad gave me some Bayer aspirin from a yellow tin. I took the medicine and rested in the car while my father visited a friend. Once I was feeling better, I got out of the car and went to the house where I thought he was. Luckily, I picked the right house. Upon entering the rectangle-shaped room, my father told me to sit on the love seat and that we would leave shortly. That day, I saw my father smoke crack. I remember trying to build up the nerve to ask my dad if I could try some, too. It was the wildest thing. As a kid, I felt like I wasn't brave because I couldn't work up the nerve to ask if I could smoke crack.

And the "Asshole Father of the Year Award" goes to... Kevin Senior.

I was a kid—what did I know? Fortunately, I returned home safely to the DMV without smoking crack, and I never told my mother what happened. Wait until she reads this!

My father would eventually return to the DMV Area—close by but so far away. To this day, I'm not sure why he moved home. I was in second grade when he returned. My stepmother, Linda, had divorced him during one of his stints in prison. In Washington, D.C., my father married his second wife, Carolyn, and they, too, would eventually divorce. My dad would once again leave DMV for Atlanta, Georgia, after being jumped by a group of men. This time, he would not return.

Despite the lack of guidance from my father, I was always an honor roll student that exhibited leadership traits at an early age. I was on the safety patrol in elementary school and took a liking to Student Government in middle school. Little did I know that I would lead the regional student government meetings I attended in middle school three years later. In the eighth grade, I faced a decision that would affect the next ten years of my life. I could either go to a high school with a great band and no JROTC Program, or a high school with a decent band and an Army JROTC Program. I chose the school with the band and the Army JROTC Program—a program I would lead in my senior year. I would also find time to play a season of football and wrestling and two seasons of baseball before my leadership responsibilities with the Prince George's Regional Association of Student Government (P.G.R.A.S.G.)

would require much more of my time. I was elected president of my sophomore class, P.G.R.A.R.S.G. President my junior year, and Student Member on the Prince George County Board of Education. I was the first student board member to have voting rights in the 17th largest school district in the nation. Unfortunately, my father was not present for any of my accomplishments or activities, but I persevered.

The approach I have used as a father is derived from how I was reared. My mother taught me to treat people the way I wanted to be treated—with dignity and respect. She taught me that my best was enough and that I could do whatever I set my mind to do.

Whether she knew it or not, she taught me what it means to sacrifice oneself for your child long before I thought about starting a family. My mother took a part-time job in a toy store during the Christmas holidays to save money to pay for my braces. She would suffer back problems from moonlighting at that toy store. She straightened shelves to straighten my teeth. Why is a mother's love often so different from a father's love? You would never know that my mother didn't complete high school because she worked so hard to better herself and care for me. She ensured that my education was supplemented with after-school and summer learning programs. It sucked to be the kid going to school after school and during the summer, but it paid off. With my mother's help, I persevered too.

The women in my family and my uncles would fill the void left by my absent father. My mom's youngest sister, Margie, would meet and marry Marshall. Marshall was from the south, with the southern flare to match. He was an Army Commissioned Warrant Officer that worked as a Federal Criminal Investigator. He taught me the mannerisms and characteristics of an honorable man. My junior year in high school was when my cousin Corey and I voluntarily uprooted ourselves from our single-parent homes and moved in with our favorite aunt and uncle. Margie was the fun aunt who traveled the world while in the military and was stationed in the DMV Area.

She and Marshall moved to the wealthiest concentration of African Americans in the United States—Upper Marlboro, Maryland, where they bought the largest house our family had ever seen. They would serve as the nucleus and the host for countless family gatherings. This would be where I would call home for my last two years of high school and my first two years of college.

Marshall would build the structure on the foundation of my life poured by my mother. As Pastor Hallback would teach me later in life, "Some things are taught, and some things are caught." Marshall was undoubtedly worthy of emulating. Long before Steve Harvey told the world, Marshall taught me that every man should own a black, a blue, a grey, and a tan suit and a blue blazer with gold buttons. He instilled the importance of buying a quality leather shoe that could be spit-shined. Margie and Marshall taught me that dinner was to be eaten at the table and that house chores were to be performed on Saturday mornings before my weekend began. Marshall took Corey and me outside one Saturday morning to demonstrate his yard manicuring standards and cut the grass path that would form the mandatory diagonal wave formation.

Marshall's standard would become my own almost a decade later. I was taught that failure to comply with the rules came with consequences. I was told to always make my bed before leaving the house. I remember leaving the house for work at the local plant nursery, forgetting to make my bed. Knowing me, I'm pretty sure that I was running late and, most likely, rushing. As a matter of fact, I know I was rushing because when I came home to grab the lunch (that I obviously forgot), I was greeted with a note on my unmade bed. *See me when you get home.—Marshall*

When I got home, although Margie was working in the kitchen, she silently slipped out, leaving only Marshall and me in the dimly lit room. The conversation was quick and to the point, followed by a week of punishment.

Marshall played a vital role in my rearing, but there would be countless other men in my life that would indirectly show me what right looks like through their actions. The men of Allen Chapel African Methodist Episcopal (A.M.E.) Church would provide practical examples of a man grounded by faith. Misters Harris, Bradford, Bobo, Johnson, Smeedly, Gumbs, and my Great Uncle Charles showed me how to be present in my home, available and giving to my church, and active in my community. These men were father figures and role models to the fatherless, but more importantly, they were obedient to God's Word. Growing up as a child, my mother ensured that I went to church every Sunday, even if she was not in attendance. The brown church van would pick me up for Sunday School. I learned that men gave of their talent, time, and tenth for the greater good. I would soon fall in step by joining the Young People Division and the youth choir. After a while, my contributions and leadership in the church were recognized, and I was selected as a Junior Steward of the church. What an honor! I was grateful for the opportunity and the responsibility that came with being an officer of the church. Allen Chapel A.M.E. Church also assisted in filling the void in my life as a critical member of the village responsible for the man that I am today.

Other members of the village responsible for rearing me were the educators who took their duties further than their job descriptions and responsibilities required. Their involvement in my life has lasted for 30-plus years and continues until this day. Mrs. Brown and McCann (student government advisor), Mr. Crouch (a social studies coordinator), Dr. Daley (Army Lieutenant Colonel Retired), and Rev. Dr. Jones (Army Colonel Retired) all pushed me to excel academically and in my extracurricular activities. Collectively, they nourished my ambitions and stretched my expectations to fit the future they knew I was capable of achieving. Under the guidance of the latter two in the Army Junior Reserve Officer Training Corps (J.R.O.T.C.), my leadership style and practices developed to serve as the foundation for a 20-year Army career.

While in college, I had an opportunity to live with my mother's brother and his family for about six months. There, I gained the finishing touches on what I perceived the role of a man should be. Uncle Eddie was a social worker at a youth detention center and pastored a church for as long as I could remember. He showed me that fatherly intrusiveness was best when driven by love and not control. Uncle Eddie married

Shirley, and they had four children, one to five years younger than me. My stay with Uncle Eddie showed me the blueprint for a father's healthy involvement in his children's lives. Uncle Eddie and Aunt Shirley instilled in their children the importance of being well-rounded and diverse. All of my cousins were required to play an instrument and a sport. Sitting down together as a family for dinner was a requirement, and being part of a family who talked about their day over dinner was my highlight. Yes, my mother formed my foundation, and Uncle Marshall built the structure of my manhood, but it was Uncle Eddie who was the example of how to apply fatherhood from a practical perspective when I started my family.

I completed my matriculation at my family's chosen institution of higher learning. My mother's brothers, Eddie and Wendell, and her sister, Margie, all attended Norfolk State University. I received my commission into the United States Army Field Artillery Corps as a 2nd Lieutenant.

Old soldiers often jokingly say that if the Army wanted me to have a wife, they would issue me one. It would be at Fort Sill, Oklahoma, where I would meet my wife and life partner. The Army issued me Danielle! We worked hard to navigate marriage challenges, but after six years in, I gave Danielle an ultimatum. I told her I felt that my life would be incomplete if we did not have children, and without children, we could not remain married. Danielle had told me she didn't desire to have children, but I had hoped she would change her mind with time.

Time doesn't change everything, as we often like to think, but fortunately for us, my wife changed her mind because of her love for me and her respect for my desire to fulfill what I just knew was one of my life's purposes. We made many attempts to start a family, but had no success. It soon became pretty apparent that there was a medical issue. I traveled to the Army's top hospital and met with their best doctors in urology, and after a very invasive test, it was discovered that I could not have children. I didn't produce sperm. I was firing blank ammunition. I still got the "bang" but without the "pow." I had a pool full of water but no swimmers. I think you get the point. This news was devastating and hard to accept. Danielle and I explored In Vitro Fertilization (IVF) again without success. However, we soon learned that God has a plan, and His plan is perfect.

Danielle and I would become licensed to foster and adopt children in the state of Texas, and our lives would change forever. Entering our lives would be a baby boy named Chance. I'd been training all of my adolescent life and through my early adult years for fatherhood, and in 2014, it was my time to apply everything that I had learned until that point. I was overjoyed to fulfill my dream of having a family.

Danielle and I had a lull in what had been a pretty rough marriage, long enough to adopt, but it did not solve our problems as a couple. In fact, expanding our family exacerbated the unaddressed issues in our marriage. It had become toxic and unbearable. Honestly, I was afraid of one of us getting hurt or locked up, and the male is usually the one hauled off because, in many situations, he is the aggressor. I realized I had been carrying around my childhood issues as they related to my parent relationship. And as far as I was concerned, Danielle had given me every right to seek a divorce from year one and almost every year following, but I stuck it out because I loved her, and I didn't want to be another divorce statistic. So, just like my parents, we argued and fought. Yelling and lack of respect for one another became the norm. My visions of fatherhood quickly diminished, and I began to contemplate the unthinkable. I was considering divorcing Danielle and leaving my family just as my father left my mother and me to fend for ourselves. Was I cursed by my grandfather's and my father's actions? My grandfather had left his family, my father had left me, and I was about to do the same thing to Chance. It would be the hardest decision of my life.

On January 3, 2017, I mustered the nerve to tell Danielle I wanted a divorce. Unfortunately, the relief of getting that off my chest was quickly met with things going from bad to worse between us. I had to get out, but could I be a good father to Chance without being a husband to Danielle? In my mind, the two were synonymous, but I was going to give it a try. Danielle and I separated in June 2017 and divorced on June 28th, 2019, and I had to adapt my vision of fatherhood to one weekend a month, a holiday, spring break, and summer. Unlike my father, however, I made it my business to support my son with child support and spend every court-ordered visit with Chance. I was determined to be the best father I could be by seizing every moment. My goal was to create good memories and not issue empty promises like the ones my dad made to me.

Dropping Chance off became harder each time, but I knew that divorcing Danielle was the only thing that would allow her to hit rock bottom and get the help she needed so that we could eventually rebuild our relationship and renew our commitment to one another.

In December 2020, Danielle allowed Chance to live with me semi-permanently. Danielle and I would later reconcile in August 2021.

If I could leave a few fatherhood feathers for your fedora, these are the points I would leave you with...

Live a life worthy of emulating; iron sharpens iron. As it's said, action speaks louder than words. Our children repeat the actions and habits we live in front of them more than our words. The actions of my village continue to have a profound effect on my life even today.

When you are a jack of all things, you may be a master of nothing. ***Know your strengths and build a village that diversifies your ability to rear a healthy and balanced child.*** Develop relationships and be involved with those that lead your child's extracurricular activities. This beneficial relationship could easily transition into mentorship and unofficial adoption into the family. I am still in relationship with those critical few from high school, 26 years later.

Instill responsibility and accountability in your children through tasks and chores. People are creatures of habit. The sooner healthy habits are started, the better. Of course, the goal is not to make your child a miniature adult or to sacrifice their childhood. Moderation and consistency are key.

Developing a relationship with your children's teachers and the school system is a must to understand your children's needs. Staying postured to supplement when needed with tutoring or other educational enhancements goes a long way. Remember, you only get one opportunity at a meaningful beginning during your child's crucial developmental phase.

Never neglect the importance of sports and their countless benefits in life. Tracks, fields, and courts are the breeding grounds for the next generation's crop of leaders. During these activities, children will learn to mediate conflict, encourage others, develop a sense of teamwork, and work together to achieve a common goal. The health benefits of an active lifestyle can also be life-altering. Therefore, I strive to diversify my son through his activities. As an example, I leverage music with sports! Chance loves football, but while his mind is in the developmental phase, to play football, he must also play the piano. His mother and I view the piano as a gateway instrument to all other musical experiences.

Fatherhood is a series of both positive and sometimes negative experiences. As fathers, we can't wait to recreate the positive experiences, spawning traditions for generations to come. Therefore, our actions must be immediate and intentional for the good of our children. The values my mother instilled in me, coupled with Uncle Marshall's mentoring and Uncle Eddie's commitment, along with the faith demonstrated by the men of Allen Chapel AME Church and the dedication of my educators, gave me all the tools I would need to navigate fatherhood.

Chance's name was not chosen by Danielle nor by me, but we kept it for many reasons. Chance gave me the opportunity to be a father, and we promised to provide him with a life better than the one he would have had in the foster care program—to create experiences that will ground him and opportunities that will take him wherever he decides he wants to go. We will teach Chance the routines that create success and become traditions for generations. I thank God for bringing my family back together and blessing me with the *Chance* to be the best father I can be.

Emery Williams Jr.

Growing up in a military family shaped Emery Williams' perspective as a global citizen. Born in Germany and having lived in three different cities over eight years, he gained the experience of living in a foreign country while learning about other cultures. He continued his education at the University of Oregon and Central Washington University. While there, he participated in football and track and developed an even greater ability to communicate and interact with people from different backgrounds and cultures.

After graduating from college, Emery taught in various educational settings, including public schools, juvenile prisons, group homes, and therapeutic hospitals for adolescents. Thirty-seven years of experience in teaching and leading in the field of special education substantiated his preparation for a lifelong career. In addition, the legal, ethical, and personal experiences enhanced his leadership skills, enabling him to impact the community. Specifically, over the past twenty years, he assisted in implementing a non-profit organization, *Youth Education and Sports Inc.* This program encourages students to participate in extracurricular activities while documenting their life experiences. In addition, the Student-Athlete/Artist Achievement Program enables community youth to focus on the skills and work ethic needed to succeed.

Emery attributes his success to the unconditional love and support of his beautiful and talented wife. He is the father of ten and has been a mentor and father figure to the hundreds of student-athletes and student-artists he has taught or coached. Combining his love of youth and gift of encouragement, Emery continually aspires to teach excellence.

CHAPTER 18

Unconditional Love

Coach Emery Williams Jr.

My journey starts as a military dependent born in Heidelberg, Germany. I am the grandson of an abandoned grandfather who, as a hobo living train-to-train from Louisiana to Missouri, landed in Mississippi, where sharecropping became his livelihood. He eloped from this form of slavery with a sixth-grade education, a daughter, and two sons, one of them my father, after losing my grandmother way too soon. My father later enlisted in the Army for a better life. This background information outlines the grit and determination passed down through the generations, shaping my character. This trait of tenacity has been honored through  the love of family, and our determination to survive, which represents our family's foundation.

My family history of trials, tribulations, and perseverance echoes the strength, dignity, and love that surrounded me throughout my childhood and youth. The erecting of the Berlin wall and the threat of World War III are in the backdrop of my birthplace of Heidelberg, Germany. During a military high alert, my father was deployed to the point of conflict, and my mother was directed to prepare to evacuate back to the United States. She was informed she would have to leave her baby boy. Preparations were being made, and my parents found a family to be surrogate parents. They agreed to take a Black baby boy to be theirs during this uncertain time. Oma and Opa, a childless German family, decided to disregard the community backlash and the social difficulties they would face by adopting me. This gesture of unconditional love has been a recurring theme in my life.

My father came from a family that worked for everything in life. He showed me that I had to work to provide for my family. His servant leadership was an ongoing adventure.

As a military family, we were very transient during my childhood and early adolescent years. My father was deployed to Vietnam, and we lived in Texas to be close to my mother's family. We lived in several states before being transferred to Germany for a second time. Our family bond grew stronger as we lived in the military family housing area. We were able to see the world when he was transferred to different bases, and I experienced traveling across the United States at a young age. The downside of moving frequently prevented me from having close friends. Growing up, I had no friendships that lasted over one year. Even as an adult, I have one or two people that I consider close friends. But my father tried to fill the free time that we had during the summer and some of the gaps that military-dependent children face. We didn't watch a lot of television. In Germany, the viewing selection was short, and if you didn't understand the German language, it was a waste of time. The after-hour adult portion was the only interesting viewing! During vacations, however, my father made sure we went on adventures exploring the history of Germany. We traveled on the Autobahn (a highway with no speed limit), went to castles, Oktoberfest, visited the Berlin Wall (it was still erected), and witnessed many of the ruined buildings, arenas, and concentration camps. The opportunity to see and experience German culture firsthand positively influenced my view of the people of Germany. We met people that invited our family to have dinner at their home, and our family had many interactions with families at community gatherings, local restaurants, and the public swimming pool. My childhood memories are full of fun and joyful experiences!

The conversations we had while traveling during our outings exposed my father's line of thought. He wanted us to see that people of color could go anywhere and be accepted with no type of fear or rejection. My father was raised in the deep south of Mississippi during Segregation. As a child, I could remember traveling across the US and being told to lie down on the floor when crossing through Alabama. The fear that my parents experienced was not visible. They tried to shield us from the prejudice that was associated with being a person of color. Growing up in Germany, I felt no type of rejection or fear because of my color. My father's desire to show us how to work, be adventurous, have fun, and see the world has directly affected the way that I have raised my kids.

We would only remain in Germany for two years. The last stop would be in Washington State when my father was transferred to Fort Lewis. Being a career military man is a very difficult lifestyle for a young father. We were often left with my mother for extended times when he was in the field or on assignment. My mother was affected because she was left alone to raise two children with minimal support. She often had to get a part-time job to help with bills and to make sure that we were provided with meals. Their relationship started to fall apart when he began to drink alcohol to help deal with his stress. I witnessed spouse abuse firsthand, which negatively affected my relationship with my father.

My parents divorced when we were in our early teenage years. I was blessed to have a loving stepfather that cared for our blended family with no hesitation. He was a family man that recently divorced and was a single father of two boys. My stepbrothers and I were playmates before either of our parents divorced. We bonded as a family through the leadership of my stepfather. I could talk with him about anything that a young man needed advice about while growing up. I am forever grateful for the love that he showed toward our family.

My biological father was a Staff Sergeant over the Mess Hall in the Army, and he was an excellent chef. He also enjoyed cooking for the family. During this last station, he served the youth that took part in the Special Olympics. I was invited to take part in serving the athletes when I experienced a life-changing event. While serving food and talking with the athletes, I was hugged by one of the female athletes. The love that I felt was unexpected. A big genuine hug given to me by an athlete with disabilities was saying "thanks for your service." This interaction changed my perspective on serving others and making a difference. At this point, I knew that I would work with children. I was called "The Pied Piper " by my mother! This was because kids from all over the area always came to the house. The kids around the neighborhood were involved with the many games and activities that I organized in our area. I continued volunteering with the Special Olympics through high school, and other students chose to participate with me!

Military dependents were provided with a variety of services specifically for children. Among them was an activity center that provided activities, tours, and events. I showed an interest in sports during elementary school and began playing football and baseball. This led to my participation in team sports throughout my junior high and high school years. I was often cut from teams because of my poor fundamental skills, but I kept trying. I was fast, and I could jump, but I was clumsy. My mother suggested that I try an instrument when I was in the fourth grade because she loved the saxophone. She bought a tenor saxophone and gave it to me. The case was so large that I struggled with carrying it to school and back home! I found some success with playing an instrument. Relatives and neighbors would ask about the big case that I was carrying and give a slight smile when I told them it was a saxophone. My skill level in sports and music increased as I progressed through school. I was asked to play my saxophone in an adult group in junior high school and later played in a select musical concert with Daryl Dragon from Captain and Tennille.

After high school, my dream of being a college football player, triple jumper, and musician was launched. I walked on to be part of the University of Oregon football team and track team. We started a nightclub band that a local radio host led. Being a student was not the focus. The desire to be successful in everything I started was my motivation. Without guidance or a true plan, I was like a rat in a maze, exploring the pathway to reach my destiny. Being a musician is truly a struggle that I experienced while attempting to be in a band during college. We had the honor of being the opening act for BB King and Ella Fitzgerald! It was an out-of-body experience, to say the least. Despite experiencing some success, I continued to enjoy helping others succeed. Taking part in rigorous collegiate sports, an extended nightlife, being a musician, and being a student were all a part of my hectic schedule.

As time passed, I had to decide what I wanted to do with my life. I wanted to continue playing music and sports, but I was at the end of my college experience. The NFL experienced a strike, so I had continuous thoughts of crossing the strike lines to try out for the league. My music career continued, but I needed a job that would pay on a regular schedule with benefits. I had always thought about serving kids since my Special Olympics experience, so I decided to go into the school system as a Special Education Teacher. My career began as a public school teacher working with behavior disorders, emotional disorders, and conduct disorders. The students thrived in my classroom. I had begun my life of service to students and families in the community.

The recognition of being a father figure came into my life relatively early. Looking at my definition of fatherhood, I understood that being an effective father required many characteristics. Among those characteristics are loving, trustworthy, dependable, a servant leader, passionate, and transparent with the ability to show weakness, strength, and emotions.

When raising children, I looked back on how my parents nurtured my sister and me, and I recalled the importance of introducing my children to the world as seen through the eyes of a child. It is important to show them the wonder and variety of endless opportunities available to them in the world. I remembered the importance of teaching children how to have fun, demonstrating involvement in the community, being a hands-on father throughout their trials and tribulations, and demonstrating how to conduct yourself when dealing with society.

Accepting the responsibility of providing security for my children through emotional support and making sure their daily needs were provided was my daily focus. The foundation of fatherhood begins with showing our children they are loved for who they are individually and unconditionally. Simply stated, fatherhood is the determination to raise kids to be better than we are.

My introduction to fatherhood began as a surrogate father to my niece, who was born to my sister, a teenage mother. One of my visits back home during my college break brought a new challenge of being an uncle. The motivation to be successful and help raise my niece became a focus. My sister would make frequent trips to New York while having Nana take care of her child, and I was compelled to help with raising my niece during summer break. The opportunity to help raise my sister's kids as a father figure increased as she eventually had four kids. She made many bad choices during this time. She struggled with taking care of her children until my mother had to rescue them from Child Protection Services. Initially, I had feelings of resentment. I had no kids of my own, and I questioned why I would have to raise my sister's kids when I was not responsible for them. My feelings changed, and I decided to step in to help the kids. It was my choice to show love and commitment to my family, nieces, and nephews that led me into fatherhood.

I began to feel the pressure of providing an example of what a good father should look like. The daily life lessons, talking with the kids about believing in themselves, how to deal with problems, and peer pressure, was overwhelming. When there were issues I didn't know how to deal with, I leaned on the examples that my parents demonstrated.

When summer came to a close, I returned to college, and my mother continued to raise the kids while I worked toward my degree. We would spend as much time together as possible during breaks or holidays, and I was intentional about taking my nieces and nephews to cultural and musical events in the community while they were adolescents.

As I mentioned earlier, although I was the father figure for my nieces and nephews, I had no children of my own. But one phone call changed that. My high school sweetheart, who left me and was pregnant during her senior year, was on the phone. I was in my last semester of college, and I was home for the summer. The conversation was one of the most difficult I had faced. She talked of the difficulties of motherhood and raising a son as a single parent. The person who she said was the father of her son was incarcerated and was not in their life. She shared that while in prison, he was required to take a paternity test for validation because he had to pay child support. The test indicated that he was not the father and cleared him of parental responsibility. I was then informed that I was the father of a four-year-old boy!

My initial emotions of joy and happiness swirled with questions of why this happened, how did I miss out on the birth and first four years of my firstborn, and is this real? Crazy thoughts mixed with feelings of confusion, anger, resentment, and my questioning if this was really happening. I had immediate feelings of guilt surrounding my not being there for him, him being raised by another man, and what conditions did he experience? Reality set in when I met my son for the first time. His beautiful eyes with a smile like sunshine confirmed that I was a dad, his dad! I now had an opportunity to have a relationship, develop a bond, create memories, and provide a home for my son.

The focus of my life turned toward being a good father and away from chasing my dreams of becoming a professional football player. Finding jobs came easily as I was on a mission to do the right thing, and my son was the motivation. I was able to rent a three-bedroom house to prepare for my son, his mother, his brother, and two rescue dogs. The dogs served as therapy dogs for the kids and their mother. They had faced very tough times as a family when they lived in Washington.

My son's adjustments were initially difficult because he had previously lived in a town that didn't have much diversity. He grew up with very few people of color and did not experience any type of cultural bias or prejudice. Now he was introduced to his newly found family and a new culture that included people from diverse backgrounds - first cousins that were mixed with Black and Latino ethnicities, White family members, and Black relatives contributed to his culture shock. We went to cookouts, swam and fished at the lake, birthday parties, and family gatherings to meet family members. He had many questions that needed to be answered about being mixed and the differences between being Black and White. I chose always to relate the differences and similarities to the reoccurring theme of love and how people are the same. It didn't take long before he felt like he was one of the family members.

My attempt to mend my relationship with the mother of my son and to start over was met with resistance. We were two people who were too young and immature to recognize the sacrifices required to raise a child. The pressure of trying to be a good father, even though I was not in a relationship with his mother, affected my efforts to build the relationship. I felt that I was not trusted to be a father to my son and his brother. There was a constant feeling that something was going on in our relationship that I could not put a finger on. I wanted to make up for lost time with my son, but I didn't know how. I decided to spend as much time as I could showing him how much I love him.

I wanted to share my life with him. I recognized that I couldn't make up for the past, so I focused on being present with my son. The decision to be present was the answer to both of our needs. He needed to have me in his life, and I needed him to allow me to be in his life. I realized that my relationship with my son was not dependent on my relationship with his mother.

My advice to fathers, spend time in the present with your children. Block out the rest of the world when possible. I learned that one-on-one time with my son was important to building our relationship.

I eventually found myself living in a three-bedroom house with my son and my niece. The stability that I provided confirmed this as the best place for the kids to live. This is the point where I began to experience the daily pressures of being a father. Raising early adolescents when they are dealing with puberty, emotions, and confusing interpersonal feelings can be very difficult. My sister was informed that she could get her kids back when she met the conditions required by the state, and both kids eventually chose to move back with their mothers. I will admit that I had conflicting feelings of emptiness and relief when they chose to go back to their mothers. But our relationship continued as I spent time with the kids on weekends and during select holidays. The kids frequently called to talk about their day and anything they wanted to talk about. I enjoyed being a father and a role model for the kids, and I had as much fun as they did when we went on outings.

Although our relationship continued, I was not emotionally strong when I had to face physical separation from my children. There were periods of time when I did not have much contact with them. I took that time to focus on myself and what I needed to improve personally, but I went through a dark and difficult period when I was alone. My spiritual beliefs were important during this time. I found myself searching for my purpose but turned my focus toward my job to escape the loneliness. I ultimately needed to decide what was important and how I wanted to live my life. For any fathers going through similar circumstances today, I would suggest focusing on your emotional well-being and building healthy self-esteem. If help is needed to rebuild yourself, seek a professional. You must be able to be vulnerable yet firm in dealing with personal feelings. As men, we have been conditioned from childhood to be strong and unemotional, so vulnerability doesn't come easy. But it's necessary and critical for our well-being and for healthy relationships.

Time brought about a change in my family when I introduced my newly pregnant girlfriend and her two children. Her two beautiful girls and our baby boy were my new family. My older son and niece accepted them as family members. There was an understanding that I had a new family, but we were all one family, even though we didn't all live together in the same house. The kids became close as they grew up together. I raised the girls as if they were my own daughters. We went to the gym and took part in activities in the community. Many times I would have them all together, seven kids - my nieces and nephews, my sons and daughters - my blended family. We would pile into the 1982 big-body Chevy Impala and go to the lake. We grew up together as I learned how to be a father. The early mornings and late nights were spent talking about school, personal relationships, personal interests, and plans. Spending personal time with the kids was a challenge. The age differences allowed me to make time for small groups of kids and some one-to-one interactions.

Providing for a large family is a difficult task when you are unprepared for the responsibilities important to raising children. The financial challenges of providing for the family's daily needs were difficult and required both parents to be employed to help meet the family's needs. I had to get two jobs just to ensure there would be enough money to sustain us until the next payday. While working two jobs, I could not be at home with the family. My "new" relationship started to experience problems because of the stress related to finances, and my absence played a big part in the ending of our relationship. My focus and priority had become how to make more money rather than being present with my family. This contributed to a severed relationship and the fact that we were no longer compatible. We chose to go our separate ways at this point, but I maintained a relationship with the kids whenever it was possible to schedule a date.

Advancing my career while serving the youth in the community became my focus. If I was going to help support my family, I would need to get a higher degree to be eligible for higher pay. A distance learning program through Cambridge College would be my only option for a master's degree. For the first time in my life, I was focused on academics. My social life became secondary, and sports and music were put aside for the goal of completing my degree. The school year began with the typical beginning activities. Then I saw her - my future wife, the mother of my four children, and The Love of My Life!

Life was no longer the same after she came into my life. We were married and later had four kids! With 36 years of teaching experience, my job is not such a big focus in my life. My family values are similar, but I have the support of my wife. My level of trust has improved over time, and parenthood responsibilities are a team effort. It takes both parents to provide for the needs of the family. Previously, I thought I had to assume most of the responsibilities of raising the kids and providing for the family. But together, we raised our children to be equipped for the future. I have learned valuable lessons from my raising my older children that I'm able to apply to my younger children. Most of all, I am more patient when disciplining my younger children.

As I continued to serve youth in the school system, I realized that not only was I raising my kids, but I was also providing fatherly support for a number of disadvantaged youth in the community. My approach was to challenge them through sports and education. As an educator, I have witnessed kids with no support at home, leaving them with feelings of helplessness and hopelessness. The increase in gang violence and cultural influences offered a bleak future for many kids. I was part of their daily lives, and they could relate to me without pressure. They would share the difficulties they faced daily. School provided a type of normalcy, but they still had to go back home and deal with dysfunctional family and community influences. I grieved over the way their lives predisposed them to negative outcomes. They witnessed firsthand killing, jail time, and drug sales in their communities. They often spoke about feeling like they had no options because they needed to help their mother meet the needs of the family.

One day, on the way to work, I had a vision of how to help and give them hope. 'The vision was to help kids start setting goals and start planning for their future at an early age. Empowering youth by helping them to focus on goals, with an emphasis on extra-curricular activities to provide motivation, was the answer! This vision inspired me to begin a non-profit to serve youth across the nation. Youth Education and Sports Inc. was born from this vision. The program helps kids to achieve at a high level through a Student Artist/Athlete Achievement program. Student artists and student-athletes are synonymous. Our approach is to reach youth in communities that need direction and motivation. We are changing the mindsets of youth and, in turn, changing communities. My heart for the kids continues to impact youth far beyond my wildest dreams.

Raising my children has been a joyful experience. I think that they would all agree on the fact that I love all of them the same. I often laugh when they describe my mannerisms and how they were disciplined. "He was strict but hands-on and patient. He took the time to listen and entertain. He's like a big kid who made sure we enjoyed childhood. He's approachable when I may be in a difficult place. He taught us to have a level of confidence and helped us to believe in ourselves. He told us that we can do anything and go anywhere with self-confidence and pride. He was a peaceful man that could show strength and gentleness. He can be depended on to be a provider, a support system, and a solid individual when times are difficult. When things seemed to break down, he encouraged us to keep the faith and to look on the bright side of life. My father depends on God to provide the way. He encourages his children to learn about God and to rely on Him by reading and applying the examples that God provides for us. Above all, my father is a loving person. He loves all his children unconditionally."

Many children believe they must fit a mold or be "accomplished" to be loved. They feel that if they have made mistakes or made poor choices, they are not loved or worthy of love. I wanted my kids to know they are loved unconditionally.

My expectations of my children match my deepest desire as a father. I want to see my children happy with their own families! While the road to happiness is often difficult while navigating through life, I encourage them to stay focused on what they want in life, and it will lead them to success in whatever they want to accomplish.

The ability to impact our children's lives and guide them through life is a one-time opportunity for which I am thankful. Likewise, I am grateful for the countless individuals that I have interacted with in the community, for they have helped to shape my vision for serving the community. That I am fortunate to be in all of their lives has been a blessing. I would like to thank each of you for allowing me to take part in your lives. Fatherhood has been a gift! The challenges have shaped the person I am today.

Lawrence U. Lane

Mr. Lane is an accomplished entrepreneur. He is married to Regenia Lane, his wife of 30 years and their family includes three adult children and three grandchildren. Mr. Lane received his B.S. degree in Business Administration. He continues to maximize his experiences and talents as a visionary to promote growth and change in the community of Garfield Heights, Ohio. Mr. Lane is the CEO and Founder of Truth & Vision Ministries, a non-profit multi-purpose performing arts and cultural center.

CHAPTER 19

Becoming a Man First, Then a Father

Lawrence U. Lane

At twenty-one, I became a father with my first child, a little girl, who I named after my eldest sister Arnita Star. Her mother and I met in church. My intentions were to impress her by attending church every Sunday and every Wednesday for bible study. We dated with close supervision for about a year and a half.

At this point in my life, however, we both married for the wrong reasons. Neither of us was ready for such a major responsibility. Honestly, we both wanted to have sex without the guilt.

With little experience, I did not know what I wanted for my life or who I wanted in my life. Eventually, the streets started calling, and other women became my interest.

Sometimes not returning home until the next day turned into leaving my new expecting bride home alone every weekend. And she NEVER let me forget it!

Word of advice: Never leave a woman alone when she is carrying your child.

The negativity she felt about me contributed to and influenced my daughter's opinion of me. Unfortunately, she never gave me an opportunity to establish a relationship or bond with my daughter on my own.

She spoke only about how I treated our marriage and how I was unfaithful. Understandably, she was angry and bitter towards me. Looking back, I know I was wrong. I was young, foolish, and unprepared to be a father. But I loved my little girl.

I provided financially for my daughter and her mother without fail. Once divorced, it became difficult to get quality time with my daughter. I was at the mercy of her mother on how often I could see her. She used my little girl to punish me.

One of the worst things a mother can do is to influence a child based on the relationship she has with their father. The father-child relationship is a separate relationship.

It prevented my daughter and me from being able to bond early.

Over the years, there were many times Star and I had arguments and extended periods when we did not speak because of our strong personalities. Star is very opinionated. At times, she would take a dig from her mom's pain, which I had inflicted, by reminding me of things her mother had told her about our relationship. However, she is more like me than any of my children.

Star has done very well, and I am immensely proud of her. After graduating high school, she joined the Air Force. She has earned two master's degrees and has traveled the world.

I have tried to make up for not being there when I was with her mother. It was my goal to celebrate each milestone in her life. I was there when she graduated from the Air Force, and for each degree she has earned. If I had the chance to do it again, I would be there from the beginning.

I feel like my eldest daughter has accomplished more with me not being a part of her life full time than my other children, who I poured so much into and who benefited from me being in the household with them every day.

Let's look at the difference: My oldest daughter's mother moved into a low-income housing project. But I raised my other children in the city of Beachwood, where the school system spends over $21,000 per student per year. In the city of Warren, where Star lived, the average system spend was $14,729 per student per year. With three more siblings in her household, Star watched her mother struggle.

My relationship with my current wife began as a friendship. She had to be the sweetest and easiest person I had met in my life. I could talk to her about sports, politics, or anything that was going on in my life. Never had I met anyone like Regenia, aka Gee, and to top it all off, she loved the Lord as much as I did.

She was engaged to someone else and was the mother of a six-month-old daughter, Jasmine. This little girl had a personality that I fell in love with.

Her hands were full with many family issues. She was a recent college graduate, doing the absolute best she could, trying to play the hand life had dealt her.

Regenia's mother had a strong addiction to drugs, and her immediate family, for whatever reason, just was not there to support her. I watched her attempt to be there for everybody in her family. To make matters worse, she was also taking care of her younger brother, who was about seven or eight, and her grandmother, who had raised her and who had suffered from a stroke that caused paralysis on her right side.

I wanted nothing to do with this dysfunctional situation. I had seen it in my family. There I was, a confirmed bachelor. I had my stuff together. Substantial savings in a 401K, driving a nice car, and living in a beautiful condo I had purchased. Not to mention, my pursuits in acting were booming. I was just getting noticed for my acting and stand-up routine. Did I want to bring all this unwanted baggage into my life? Looking back, it was worth it. My wife was worth it, and being a father was worth it.

Regenia and I continued to talk about the problems she was going through. She was so frustrated. Her engagement did not work out, and

I was glad about that. I could relate to what she was going through with her family, and I wanted to help her out of a tough situation.

One day she called me terribly upset, telling me her brother, Lil Larry, had a severe toothache and there was no one to take him to the dentist. "Do you think you can help me out?" She knew I had flexibility with my job. I had only met him briefly, but I had seen how his circumstances affected him. "Of course," I said.

He was in terrible pain when I picked him up. I remember thinking, he has all these uncles and aunties. Why weren't they there? He was crying. I felt so bad for this young man. I looked at his feet, his shoes, and his clothing, and I knew he needed someone in his life. Someone that would help him figure this thing out. I understood. I thought about my past, and this made me cry as well.

Gee's mother was the funniest individual I had ever met. If you were to meet her, you could not help but like her. I thought a lot of this woman. Regenia moved with her mother to help her remain clean and free of drugs. However, her mom could not do it. She started using the rent money multiple times to support her habit. Her mom was successful many times on her journey to recover from addiction, but she died unexpectedly in her sleep from a brain aneurysm. I had grown to love her mother very much.

I was determined not to get involved in Gee's problems with her family. I did not want to go down that road. But I could not turn my back on her daughter and her little brother. I had also fallen in love with Regenia. She was in a tough situation that she did not create but carried the full responsibility. I was also harboring the rejection I had experienced at an early age from not having my father in my life.

Prior to all this happening, I was preparing to leave Cleveland. I was doing stand-up while also involved in radio and acting. I had just completed a play for the Marvin Gaye Story, where I portrayed Berry Gordy, and I was getting rave reviews. Even with so much to look forward to, I just could not turn my back on Regenia or these two babies.

I started spending time with Lil Larry to be the needed male figure in his life. It was obvious he had not been a priority to anyone. Many issues traumatized him, including getting bullied in school, and he was having a tough time focusing. Teachers were suggesting giving him Ritalin, but I was dead set against that. I felt all he needed was someone to help him through these hard years.

I started looking for a three-bedroom home for us. Still, in my mind, this was temporary. Just to get them on their feet. Then I would move on. I had a goal of being a comedian and actor and getting the Screen Actors Guild (SAG) card. I was that good, and I was determined.

Christmas was around the corner. I wanted to build her brother's confidence and let him know we loved him. I spoiled him that Christmas with a PlayStation and new clothes. He was so happy! I remember, with tears in his eyes, he asked, "Will you be my dad?" Wow, that blew me away. From that moment, I was all in.

Now Jasmine, Regenia's daughter, was a different story. She was mean as hell and wanted nothing to do with me. But I did not give up. I made it a point to show Jasmine I was all in. That even though I was not her biological father, I would assume the role of her dad.

Gee was also going through the challenges of trying to get child support from Jasmine's father, who wanted nothing to do with her - his firstborn child. I told Gee that I did not believe any man that knows he has a child would not want to be a part of that child's life. So, I asked if she would let me speak with him.

The deal was going to be: tell him he had every right to see his daughter. If he wanted to be a part of her life, we could work it out. I also gave him another choice. If he did not want to be a part of her life, I would adopt her. However, he could not see her again, and he no longer would have to pay child support. I never thought he would take the deal. I watched as a sinister look came over his face. He told me some type of story about how this whole situation occurred. That day, I lost all respect for this man. He agreed to me adopting his child.

I realized there was no leaving now. Regenia informed me she did not want to have any more kids, and I was fine with that. I figured the two, Jasmine and Lil Larry, were enough for me.

However, God had other plans. After we had been together for four years, she informed me she was pregnant with our son. She was upset, not wanting another child. I remember it like it was yesterday.

She said these words to me, "Are you going to be here? I don't want to do this alone."

"I got you. This is our family. I will not leave." I remember looking at my little family and feeling so proud. There were concerns, however. I pushed them to the wind because I knew they needed me. Twenty-nine years later, I am still here. I kept my promise.

On September 20, 1996, our son Jordan was born. I had gone through the entire pregnancy with Regenia, and I was in the delivery room. I was there! If you have never watched a child come into this world, it is the most beautiful thing you can imagine. I had my son, and I was going to be the best father I never had.

When they placed my son, Jordan Lawrence, in my arms, it was a love I have never experienced in my life. It resonated through each bone and every cell in my body. I remember crying from pure joy.

When we brought him home, I took care of everything. I took off work, and I told Regenia, "Rest. I got him." I changed diapers and bathed him. Everyone that came to visit had to wear a mask. None of that kissing on him. Not my son.

After three years, Regenia and I decided it was time to marry. Jordan was the ring bearer. Jasmine was the flower girl, and Lil Larry was the best man. I finally had the family I had longed for. It felt great. I remember it being one of the best times of my life. This completed me.

We would vote on everything, from dogs to toys. Our son, Jordan, stayed in trouble. So, I set up a court system where I was the judge, his sister was his attorney, his mom the prosecutor, and Lil Larry the bailiff. We would have court to judge him for things he had done. Also, giving him a chance to explain himself and me a chance to understand what he was thinking. Gee would decide his punishment if we found him guilty. Secretly, I hoped this would inspire one of them to become an attorney.

I treated each of them equally. Even though Jordan was my natural son, there was no favoritism. I made sure they all understood that. I genuinely loved each one equally.

One time, my son made an ugly comment to his sister about finding her daddy because I was his. I explained to him how wrong that was. I hugged Jasmine and reminded her she was even more special because I chose her. She had a special love. I wiped the tears from my eyes and hugged her again.

I noticed Jasmine was dealing with a lot of emotions, and her confidence was suffering. I had to do something, so I talked to her mother about an idea I had to give her confidence.

The living room was arranged like a castle. I informed everyone of their roles. My wife was going to be my queen, and I was the king. We were going to anoint a Princess. I bought Jasmine a beautiful dress and a beautiful crown with a cape.

I cooked her favorite royal feast. When she got home, the family led her into the living room, which was now my castle.

I bought a plastic sword. I took the sword and tapped her on each shoulder, and said, "From this point on, we will know you as the Sugar Princess. You have the power to make important decisions for your brother and uncle. However, you can never hold your head low." That was the last time she ever did. Boy, did I create a monster!

I will never forget when she graduated from high school. I yelled at the top of my voice, "That's my Sugar Princess!"

I always had a side business, so I taught Lil Larry how to form and operate a business. I instilled his confidence in believing he could do anything he put his mind to. Lil Larry was a fast learner. I taught him the importance of saving, and while still in high school, he saved money for his first car, a red Nissan Pathfinder. I remember getting it painted and giving him the keys. That was something else I wished my dad had done for me. In my mind and heart, Lil Larry was my eldest son.

I have learned that becoming a father is secondary. First, you must become a man.

Fatherhood is a lifelong commitment to understanding and patience. A learning process that will continue throughout your life and your child's life. Being a father may mean your child is not a part of your DNA, but you will give, expecting nothing in return, and love unconditionally.

The worst pain I have ever experienced in life is never knowing my father or any man I could consider a father figure. An immature man, someone who I thought was my father, made a massive impact on my life.

At about eight or ten years old, my mom was in an on-and-off-again relationship with my sister's father, who I had assumed was also my father.

We had taken a trip to visit him, and I could finally meet the man that had been a figment of my imagination. I wanted a father so badly that when asked by friends about my dad, I would say he was in the armed forces; one of many lies I would tell from the embarrassment of not knowing my father.

Several cousins and other relatives were with their fathers. I could see the love each one shared, and I wanted a father in the worst way.

My sister's father would pay me no attention. He would pick up my sisters and love on them. I watched as he hugged each one, and I longed for some of the attention.

I was confused about why this man was not excited to see me. He later went to the store, and when he returned, he lined all the children up, including my cousins, from the tallest to the shortest.

He was giving out boxes of Cracker Jack popcorn, and I loved Cracker Jack because of the toy inside the box. So, this could be a forgiving moment if he gave me a box of Cracker Jack. At this point, I couldn't care less about being hugged.

He started with the tallest and worked his way down. When he got to me, he bent down and whispered in my ear, "You are not mine.

You're too damn black. Go find your daddy. He'll give you some Cracker Jack. You get none here, buddy."

I was crushed, but more embarrassed because of everything I had made up about him and how I had bragged about his automobile. As these thoughts ran through my head, not wanting to be seen, I played it off and just walked away. My older sister overheard and asked what he said to me. I repeated the painful words with tears.

My sister ran into the house and told my mom. A big fight started, which added to me thinking I had caused the ending of a good time. This incident created something that lived with me for years, as it would be much later in life before I would deal with it. I made sure I did not repeat this with any of my children.

I never missed an opportunity to tell our children how much I loved them, to hug them, and give them everything I had imagined my father would have done for me. This made the biggest impact on my life

I found my real father through www.ancestry.com. It was January 15, 2022. The man is still alive at 94 years old. His birthday is January 30, and he lives in Maryland, where my eldest daughter now lives. They have never met, but I reached out to him.

I learned I have several siblings. But again, I was rejected. They wanted nothing to do with me. This would lead me to deal with issues I could not face at eight. It would also put me in the hospital with a mild heart attack.

I have learned that you can only be who you are, and your child will only be the person they are. Unfortunately, parents do not have a playbook. You can give a child all the newest gadgets or designer clothes and enroll them in the best schools, yet still, sometimes they will find fault or not appreciate the sacrifices made.

If you have done the best that you knew how, don't feel guilty. They will return. A good apple does not fall far from the tree.

There is a saying: God takes care of babies and fools. He took care of you. He will take care of your children as well.

If given another chance, I would not give so much so quickly. I would let them go through more to learn. After all, experience is the best teacher. I recognize in hindsight that from my pain of not having a father, I overcompensated. I should have focused less on material things and more on the intangible lessons life presents.

My kids say I spoiled them. They knew Daddy would get whatever they wanted. They also knew I loved them.

Today, Lil Larry operates his own business, has a beautiful girlfriend, and they are expecting their first child. He has done well, and I am extremely proud of him.

As for our daughter, Jasmine, I wish we had dealt with some things we noticed from her at an early age. She finds fault in most things my wife and I have done. She can be very disrespectful to her mother and me, but she is always right in her mind. Nevertheless, I love her.

I'm afraid she is the one child who has hurt me the most. She has caused the most heartache and money. Because she was always so special to me, I thought we would be much closer. Sadly, that did not happen. I do not hold any resentment toward her. She has a right to feel the way she does. However, I now understand that I did the best I could for her.

In August 2020, I almost lost my son, Jordan. Two young thugs attempting to break into his friend's apartment shot him and his friend multiple times. Sadly, his friend was killed.

When Jordan was a newborn baby, I took him outside, lifted him to the sky, and gave him back to the Lord. I knew I could not protect him the way my Lord and Savior could. Nobody but Jesus protected Jordan that night. Detectives told us that our son had died, but a seasoned officer responded to the call and revived him.

So far, he is doing okay. Although he is still in my house, I'm glad he is alive. I grieve for the family of his friend, who lost their son.

It's important to give back, and I am always trying to be a father figure to young men. I founded Truth and Vision, a nonprofit organization designed to support young adults that do not have a relationship with their father, do not know their father, and need a male mentor. We help them understand the fundamentals of entrepreneurship through mentorship while mentoring the beginning phase of becoming a man.

We also give young adults alternatives to college. College is not the best option for everyone. For many years, society focused on college as the only path to success. When in fact, many successful people did not attend college. Of course, I am not suggesting that college is not a necessary tool. Education of any kind is always valuable. We provide awareness of other avenues to success.

In comparison, there are also many ways to be a father, even if you have never had a father in your life or children of your own. We are dealing with a new age of problems. It is important to understand being a father sometimes may mean being taken out of your comfort zone and asked to sacrifice to help a child in need. Someone that a child can see themselves in, as well as someone that cares.

In the words of George Herbert, "One father is more than a hundred schoolmasters."

Lawrence U. Lane
A father and proud of it.

Acknowledgments

I sincerely thank God for the vision of this anthology, and I honor the many human angels who helped me bring this book to life.

As with everything I've done in my lifetime, this book would not have been possible without the belief, commitment, patience, and unwavering love and support of many gifted people to whom I am enormously grateful.

My gratitude begins with my husband. TJ, my love, my partner of 30+ years, and the most loving, funny, and committed father a child could ever ask for. I love you, and Logan is fortunate to call you Dad. TJ, sometimes I can't believe I get to be married to you; you're definitely the husband I imagined and more. Our life together has stood the test of time and is still unfolding. I am so proud of us. I eagerly yet patiently await the many priceless adventures to come. Thank you for your help and support with this book. Thank you for sharing your story, reading chapters, listening to me think out loud the best you can, as you've done so often, and encouraging me not to give up during the most difficult, challenging, and scariest time of my life. TJ, you're such an amazing person. I love you with my whole heart, and always will be forever yours.

Joining forces with powerful women will always be a way of life for me and holds a special place in my heart. Why? It gives me a rare exposure to the strength and resilience of that individual woman. I was privileged to work with two phenomenal women on this enormous project. It was a gift to work with confident, compassionate, and courageous women.

To my publisher, Kim Roundtree. Thank you for your willingness to collaborate with me from day one. Kim, you brought your keen intellect, sound advice, generosity, and dedication to stay the course with me. Your belief in my vision made all the difference. Your professionalism, extra time spent, and expertise as a publisher were insightful and superb. Every author should be so fortunate.

Then, there is my editor, Toni Fant. Let me first start by saying there is absolutely no way that I could have completed this book in my lifetime without you sharing your incredible gift with all of us. I simply adore you. Toni, your enthusiasm, energy, and passion for what you do made me 100% sure that you were a perfect fit for this project. Toni, you certainly delivered! Your editorial expertise and creative vision for this project showed up in your ferocious eye for detail in every line written. Your editing, multiple drafts, making critically helpful suggestions to each author, and exuding patience, calm, wisdom, encouragement, and good cheer while offering rigorous, intelligent, and incredibly useful feedback stretched each author to grow as a writer. Your intensity made us better as people and in print. You helped make this a far better book than it otherwise would be. Thank you, and we're honored you shared your gift with us.

I am absolutely sure that everything in life is better when it's shared. My heart is full, and my eyes are filled with joyful tears as I pen these thoughts and feelings about the 21 gentlemen and courageous fathers that said "Yes" to collaborate and make my vision come to life. I am eternally grateful to each of you! Thank you for your commitment, dedication, and courage to authentically accept and embrace the task of sharing your personal stories with the world, with the intent to help and heal and put good energy into this world. I am firsthand a recipient of healing from all of you! Thank you for staying the course with me and showing me love and unwavering support during this journey. There are no words that I can write to express my feelings about how you have kept my vision alive and me so hopeful over the last year. I highly respect each and every one of you, and I'm so proud to have walked this path with you. I know this book has changed us all for the good, and that's just the beginning of what God has in store for us all. Thank you! You've given me a reason to be hopeful for stronger families, beautiful lives, and a prosperous healthy community.

Tyra

Made in United States
Orlando, FL
22 October 2023

38129658R00170